Misdirection

Misdirection

Opera Production
in the Twentieth Century

A. M. NAGLER

1981   Archon Books

© A. M. Nagler 1981

First published 1981 as an Archon Book, an imprint of The Shoe String Press, Inc., Hamden, Connecticut 06514

Printed in the United States of America

The original German edition was published in 1980 by Schäuble Verlag, D 7888 Rheinfelden, as number 16 in the series, Theater in our Time, under the title, *Malaise in der Oper: Opernregie in unserem Jahrhundert.*

This book was originally written in German and was translated by Johanna C. Sahlin.

Library of Congress Cataloging in Publication Data

Nagler, Alois Maria, 1907–
Misdirection: opera production in the twentieth century.

Includes index.
CONTENTS: Don Giovanni.—Così fan tutte.—The magic flute.—Fidelio.—[etc.]
1. Opera—Production and direction—History and criticism.   I. Title.
ML1700.N33   782.1′07′3   80-27000
ISBN 0-208-01899-9

To Erna

Contents

Cadenza

The hero of this improvisation is an average citizen in a better-than-average tax bracket. He also is an opera buff who partly subsidizes his monthly attendance at a questionable musical pleasure with his tax money. In short, he has a subscription to the opera.

One evening we find him again in his wonted seat where he ponders the meaning of the show curtain, painted with Chinese motifs, which blocks the view of the stage during the overture of the *Magic Flute*. Irritated, he closes his eyes to devote his full attention to the music. The poor man has not had time to read Felsenstein's "fairy tale" in the playbill. Only later, as he catches up on his reading in bed, does the meaning of the far-fetched chinoiserie become clear to him. But by then it is time to go to sleep.

Another evening in the same orchestra seat. This time, during the overture of *Così fan tutte*, the attention of the undaunted viewer is directed to a clock which, suspended above the proscenium, points to the hour of three. Our man knows that it is time to expect from the stage director, in the course of the evening, further surprises for which Da Ponte had not provided. In any event, it is 9:30 P.M. stage time when the merry farce ends. And it is really too late to leaf through the program in which the director, no doubt, had defended his idea.

Again, and not for the last time, our connoisseur occupies his comfortable seat. Nevertheless, he feels uneasy when he is confronted with a *Freischütz* scenery dominated by a defoliated forest. However, during the first intermission the program notes enlighten him: the horrors of the Thirty Years War have necessarily left their traces also on the German woods. Being a German citizen, our man fails to feel responsible for the defoliation of Vietnam. But on the stage there is also an extra portraying a cripple; no doubt, a war victim. That suffices to sour our viewer's pleasure in Weber's romanticism.

Before falling asleep, our subscriber, once more offended by the process of alienation, wonders when he first became the victim of directional arrogance in the opera. It seems a long time ago, a "thousand years" have passed by quickly, since he attended a performance of *The Flying Dutchman* that, from beginning to end, deviated from the familiar. Already the overture had an unusual, brassy sharpness. They had played the first, the Dresden version, which Wagner subsequently disowned, and there was no transfiguration at the end of the overture nor at the end of the opera. What Wagner had rejected was presented, and his ultimate scenic visions were ignored. This brings us to the center of our theme and the subject of this book: modern opera direction.

Our subscriber, to be sure, is not discouraged. Again and again he hopes that at last there will be a production which allows him to succumb to the magic of opera. The condition for that, however, is that the responsible magicians should know their craft, and only a few of them do. Günther Rennert, Otto Schenk, Oscar Fritz Schuh, Rudolf Hartmann—these are the men to whom we owe indelible operatic memories for they regaled us with unforgettable festive evenings. With their artistic sense of responsibility they proved themselves masters of that "impossible work of art" called opera.

To be sure, such theatrical feasts are exceptional and usually reserved for gala occasions. As we trace the stage history of some operas frequently revived in our century, such hours of glory will be gratefully acknowledged. But we also must be prepared to settle our accounts with a considerable number of counterfeiters, that is, with tone-deaf stage directors who seem to suffer from an ailment which can be correctly diagnosed as lack of confidence in the original score.

Oskar Bie, also an opera buff, once wrote of the opera: "Nothing could be more perfectly conceived than this combination of so many beautiful arts, and therefore we cannot expect absolute perfection in execution."[1] The following essays deal with these imperfections and weigh the imperfect appearance against the total work of art as conceived. The choice of these ten operas was determined by the prevailing interest contemporary directors have shown in them. *The Ring* was not included. Its depressing *via dolorosa* from Hitler-Bayreuth to Chéreau's iconoclasm—i.e., from the grotesque to the absurd—would require a separate study that could only confirm our diagnosis.

The present panorama of more or less current opera direction is essentially based on the personal experiences of the author, who has been witness to triumphs and defeats in numerous opera houses. Wherever personal impressions were lacking, the seasoned theater historian relied on reports of critical contemporaries. It is unavoidable that some partial readers will miss the record of a performance they cherish among their memories. For every opera under scrutiny, additional instances, favorable or unfavorable, could be cited. *Sapienti sat.* I readily admit that the following pages are taken from a very subjective log which the traveler kept for many years in fair weather and foul. The conclusions are not exactly encouraging. There is no doubt: the present practices in production lead to discord in the operatic organism. This process has been in motion ever since Stanislavsky turned to opera and agonized in the attempt to teach his Rodolfo "natural" acting, while the singer labored to cope with the vocal demand of *"Che gelida manina."* The directorial virus became virulent in Germany during the twenties. The decisive esthetic and sociopolitical battles, into which opera was also drawn, were and are fought in the vigorous German operatic arena. *Attacca!*

11

Don Giovanni

Let us begin our diagnostic history of stage productions with the "opera of all operas" (E. T. A. Hoffmann), which looks back on a stage career (first smooth, then rough) of two hundred years. For Mozart's contemporaries there was nothing puzzling in this opera; they were not bewildered by its designation as a *dramma giocoso*. It was left to our century to discover in this score conundrum upon conundrum, to create confusion in an admittedly complex cosmos.

Gustav Mahler, whose star shone in the early years of this century, sat at the harpsichord of the Vienna Hofoper on 21 October 1905, and from there conducted and directed his new production. Alfred Roller, a cofounder of the Wiener Sezession, was in charge of the scenery. Mahler would have no dealings with a dramma giocoso, Mozart's opera buffa. He saw the opera in a completely tragic light. Hence he omitted the final sextet, and only Richard Mayr's Leporello was allowed a few tame jokes.

But the sensation of the evening was not Mahler's tragic Mozart, it was Roller's scenic concept of it: side "towers" and a stage without wings. In the meantime we have become used to such a stage, have even raised it to the rank of an epoch-making invention, but the contemporaries grumbled.

Roller envisioned on both sides of the stage high, movable towers which formed a sort of inner proscenium and could reduce or enlarge the stage area by being retracted or advanced. In certain scenes these permanent flanking towers formed an entirely neutral frame. But their windows and doors could, with the aid of anterior steps, also suggest the interior of houses. The illusion of a specific locale was obtained primarily through exchangeable backdrop vistas.

The first scene, a park in front of the Commendatore's house. The backdrop was not painted but rather made of velvet, the sky of blue, the cypresses of black velvet; the stars were punched-out holes. Don Giovanni's garden was reminiscent of the Villa d'Este in Tivoli: a sun-gilt palace façade against an intense blue sky. In front of it, trimmed hedges and an abundance of flaming red roses. Luminous scarlet dominated the ballroom decorated with tapestries. The *atrio terreno in casa di Donna Anna* (act 2, scene 2) was especially impressive: a tremendous, dark, rectangular door, one rectangle within the other, one blacker than the other. Mahler insisted that the musicians shade the lamps on their music stands until one wing of the portal opened and a blinding shaft of light fell across the stage as the torchbearers entered. The graveyard lay in ashen moonlight. Stars sparkled in the sky. The marble equestrian statue was framed by three-dimensional tombs. A black wall with a life-size portrait of the Commendatore formed the background for Anna's F-major aria. At the end, the Don in white brocade dined in a glaring red hall before being devoured by hellish fires. (Roller's initial idea, that the sinner should be swallowed up in waves of black velvet, as though darkness were engulfing him, was evidently not carried out.)

Mahler had to become reconciled to Roller's relief stage before he finally committed himself to it, though not without reservations. He called Roller's innovation "a stage on which everything only insinuates, nothing 'is.' " He did not encourage the scene designer to continue his experiments. Roller divulged Mahler's reasons: "The attention of the audience must remain focused on the music and must not be distracted by arguments about the scenery."[1] And, indeed, controversy arose about Roller's scenic solutions. The audience was confused when the stage designer left the nineteenth century behind and courageously strode into the twentieth. Even such a devoted Mahlerian as Richard Specht, Mahler's first biographer, mutinied, claiming that the towers were not illusionistic, whereas the backdrops marked a clear-cut localization. This resulted in a stylistic inconsistency. "A pulling hither and yon of the imagination," Specht said, and continued: "This schizophrenic exercise demanded of the viewer's imagination during the performance really was something disquieting, at least somewhat strenuous, and finally fatiguing."[2] Bruno Walter found Roller's towers "altogether too stylized," and what went on between them un-Morzartian. He pointed out that for the champagne aria Roller had on the stage a garden with rose beds, whose strident red was not consonant with Mozart's "subtly colored instrumentation."[3]

Roller managed to change decors without disruptive pauses. None of the alterations required more than twenty or thirty seconds. Incidentally, this was not the first attempt to master, without wings or arches, the eleven localities required by the libretto. In Munich's Residenztheater (1896) Ernst Possart for the first time set in motion Lautenschläger's revolving stage for *Don Giovanni*. The audience was fascinated by this technical innovation but diverted from the opera by the "merry-go-round."

In the "Little House" of the Stuttgart Royal Court Theater, stage designer Bernhard Pankok created (1909) a permanent proscenium which continued the architectural style of the auditorium. The stage was narrowed, widened, or opened up in full (ballroom, banquet scene) with the aid of a black traveler curtain or colored backdrops. The two-act form of the opera was retained, and each act was played in seven scenes, without long waiting periods.

When Ernst Lert prepared his *Don Giovanni* in Leipzig (1917), he was enthralled by Kierkegaard's *Either/Or*. To that

15

philosopher Don Giovanni was "the incarnation of the flesh" (a tautology), an "expression of the demoniac, insofar as it is governed by sensuality." There was no doubt in Lert's mind: *Don Giovanni* was a "Bacchus myth," a "Dionysian tragedy."[4]

"Sensuous intoxication" characterized the *Don Giovanni* productions in the years after the First World War. Unfortunately, the available singers lacked charisma: there was a dearth of "bacchantic" heroes on the stage. The Portuguese baritone Francisco d'Andrade, whose demoniacally elegant Giovanni had enchanted Europe for years and who was considered ideal for the title role, had died in 1921. It was now up to the stage designers to create a milieu of Dionysian exuberance. To that end the baroque style seemed predestined. Oscar Strnad fled into the baroque in order to "activate" the stage area. Max Slevogt (Dresden, 1924) invented his own "baroque" when he gave his Don a stage ballroom which had to represent "the embodiment of enormous *joie de vivre*." Slevogt, who could not forget the d'Andrade whose portrait he had painted, was concerned with the "tremendous gaiety and elasticity of the hero who turned every situation, be it good or bad for him, into a source of amusement and a pleasure for himself. Conscious of his prodigious life force, he is not inhibited by any morality, or by any law, and for him his fellow men exist solely so that he may have his fun and games with them."[5] For the first scene Slevogt was content with a staircase and a grating against a somber nocturnal sky. Then the inn came into view and Giovanni's house with its park, whence, "like a robber baron from his castle," he could survey everything and always be on the spot. The statue of the Commendatore had superhuman dimensions. For the final scene, the painter first provided candlelight, then darkness, during which the banquet hall became transparent and displayed a grimacing devil with claws. Finally, light dawned for the ordinary day of the people liberated at last from the Don's disruptive influence.

In Berlin (Staatsoper unter den Linden, 1923) the decorations by Hans Poelzig melded architecture (his profession) and flora into "ornamental contours." His aim was to trace the "lines of Mozartian music" in his scenery. What he overlooked was that

Don Giovanni

Mozart's lines were perfectly straight and resisted Poelzig's scroll-work. But then, in a state of "sensual intoxication" a greal deal can be overlooked.

The bacchanalian intoxication was at last stopped by Otto Klemperer's Berlin production (Kroll Oper, 1928). Ewald Dülberg, whose cubistic extravaganzas will occupy us in a different context, provided the scenery. He resurrected Roller's interior proscenium, equipped with balconies which were used repeatedly throughout the opera. A black drop curtain could reduce the depth of the stage. Behind it, preparations were made to disclose a few sparse set pieces. If the early 1920s offered a plethora of "atmosphere," one could now speak of dearth and monotony. Klemperer went about his business in the pit with his characteristic severity, dryness, clarity, tautness: more rhythm than resonance. There was very little trace of a *dramma giocoso*. When a cerebral conductor and a Bauhaus architect join forces, one should not expect a bacchanalia.

Next our guided tour takes us to Austria, where we shall first pause in Salzburg. There, in the shadow of the composer's birthplace, we may hope to encounter efforts aimed at authenticity. Where else, if not here, could we anticipate perfection? But, as it turns out, Salzburg was the site for costly and disastrous productions, disappointing to the Mozart connoisseur.

There were three possible locations for the Salzburg entrepreneurs: the Festival Playhouse (Old or New) and the Rocky Riding School. Sins were committed on all stages, though no objections could be voiced to what went on in the orchestra pit, where either Furtwängler or Karajan presided. Furtwängler conducted while O. F. Schuh produced *Don Giovanni* (1950) in the Old Festspielhaus. An architect, Clemens Holzmeister, undertook the decor, which led to discords between director and designer. From the beginning, Schuh had been against the choice of the architect and was now unable to realize his own production ideas in Holzmeister's settings. "The singers looked so disproportionate and truly lost in the vast space that a dramatic development on the stage was no longer feasible."[6] The production had trouble measuring up to

17

the music. Schuh retired for a time, while Furtwängler and Holzmeister remained to collaborate (1953) on a production in the
Rocky Riding School. Twenty years earlier Holzmeister had
erected a medieval city for Reinhardt's *Faust* in the open-air arena.
This time he built a part of Seville on a polyscenic stage. The audience viewed the following scenes of action, left to right: the entrance to an elevated terrace of Donna Anna's house; a staircase to
a bridge leading over a city gate; the inn, for Elvira; a stair to the
cemetery with the church façade; finally, Don Giovanni's palace
and pleasure garden with pavilions and fountains; and right in
front of the orchestra pit, a statue of the Madonna. Understand-
ably, the stage director Herbert Graf felt he was the legitimate
heir of Max Reinhardt. While Furtwängler tried hard to keep
faith with Mozart, the ghost of Belasco had his fling on the stage,
suggesting to the singers, caught up in a topographical maze,
stratagems that might get them out of their spatial predicaments.

In 1960 Don Giovanni and Schuh moved back into the Old
Festspielhaus, this time with Karajan in the pit. Teo Otto was in
charge of the decors, much to the satisfaction of the stage director,
who had decided on a tragic interpretation. For this production
Schuh emphasized the "Christocentric" point of view which dominates Da Ponte's libretto, leaving no doubt as to the existence of
God and the devil and that the world is governed by eternal laws.[7]
That is, a myth culminating in divine retribution. Otto created a
sort of surrealistic Spain, decadent but not without fascination,
though contrary to every note that Mozart wrote. Seville became
a city of ruins, a refuge for bombed-out people. Schuh's biographer commented: "The world of Don Giovanni, his house and
what one might call his ambiance is fitted with mirrors and a shin-
ing golden background—the diabolical abode of a lecher, hinting
simultaneously at destruction and temptation, a sort of permanent
ante-hell."[8] That does not sound much like Mozart.

A few months before the Salzburg revival, Schuh had produced
the opera in Cologne. There Caspar Neher created an abstract
stage design which evoked no association with Spain. Three ramps
led up to a raised acting platform. A few monochrome Craigian

"screens," which could be moved and exchanged, defined the setting dominated by a stylized sun ever present as a symbol of a higher order and a fateful reign.

In 1968 it was von Karajan's turn to suffer defeat as a director at the New Festspielhaus in Salzburg. Günther Schneider-Siemssen designed a voluptuous Spain, again in the most somber hues. The gigantic statue of the Commendatore, which accented the graveyard in archaic dimensions, was indeed memorable. Much less impresive was the ghost when it finally appeared as a projection. Now and again too many visual effects did not conform to the score. For example, during Zerlina's aria, a musical number of decidedly intimate nature, the listener was distracted by seeing other rustic visitors ramble through the vast park. There was much that did not go with the text. In the first scene, the Commendatore had a house, from which he emerged for the duel. But Giovanni and Anna did not enter from that house, where after all the preceding event had taken place. (Anna later says: *"nelle mie stanze."*) Instead, they came—from the park! Evidently, the scenic changes were rather complicated and made it necessary that some of the more important arias be sung "in concert" in front of a drop curtain.

A few impressions from Vienna: *Don Giovanni* was one of the operas with which the reopening of the restored State Opera House was celebrated in 1955. (Incidentally, *Don Giovanni* was the first work performed in 1869 at the opening of the Hofoper.) The trio Böhm-Schuh-Neher supervised the new production. They had decided on a unit set that would have to serve all scenes. At times, this overtaxed the imagination of the audience. Two semicircular staircases led to a sort of a bridge above a central portal. Left and right downstage, buildings were suggested. Chandeliers provided a festive mood when needed. But in general a gray monotony weighed heavily on the performance, and the curtains in front of which the great arias were sung seemed to be makeshift solutions, especially since technical miracles had been expected from the newly constructed stage.

By 1967, Vienna was ripe for a new *Don Giovanni*, the result of a collaboration between Otto Schenk and Luciano Damiani. This time the accent was on the *giocoso*. A mood of commedia dell'arte, playfulness, light irony, some improvisation, and some burlesque not far removed from Hanswurst, dominated the performance. It evoked the Vienna premiere of 1788—by no means the worst reminiscence.

In 1972, when Franco Zeffirelli took on the directing and design chores, the colors darkened once more. The somber, autumnal decors exuded a faint odor of decay. Incidentally, Zeffirelli's romantic fantasy had previously been tried out in a Covent Garden *Don Giovanni* (final form, 1963).

Our contemporary directors feel impelled to fathom the "basic situation" of an opera. Let us join this game, and we arrive at the following reconstruction: Donna Anna at first thought the nocturnal visitor in her room was Don Ottavio. The intruder had concealed his identity. But soon the *dama* discovered that the *galan* was not her fiancé. The disguised man tried to embrace her, covering her mouth with one hand while rendering her immobile with the other arm until she mustered enough strength to tear herself loose and shout for help. Thereupon the unknown villain took to his heels, pursued by Donna Anna screaming *"traditore"* ("traitor") and *"scellerato"* ("criminal"). Her cries for vengeance brought on the stage her father, who was done in forty beats later.

In his novella *Don Juan*, E. T. A. Hoffmann elevated Donna Anna to the role of key figure. Hoffmann's imagination, as he himself admitted, changed his interpretation of the nocturnal scene "without any regard to the libretto." In his story, Hoffmann was convinced that Don Giovanni had reached his goal with Donna Anna: "When the Don fled, the deed was accomplished. The fire of a superhuman sensuality, a blaze from hell flowed through her innermost being and made all resistance useless." Donna Anna embraced the irresistible intruder with "voluptuous madness."[9] This is another Hoffmannesque fantasy, one of his "night pieces," far removed from the libretto. What was poetic license with Hoffmann became scholarly prejudice with the musicologist. In his Mozart book, Alfred Einstein arrived at the conclusion that Anna was "a victim of the hero," who, "in the dark of night, disguised as Don Ottavio, had his will."[10] There is nothing of that in the libretto. We are not entitled to assume that Donna Anna lies to her fiancé (in recitative no. 10) when she tells him what happened in that fateful hour.

When Walter Felsenstein started on his production (Komische Oper, East Berlin, 1966), he had long pondered the relationship between Giovanni and Anna. He was persuaded that the Don did not have his way with the Donna. There is nothing in Da Ponte of either voluntary surrender or rape. Anna talks about the violation of her honor, and according to the Spanish *pundonor* she is entitled to make such an accusation. So far we are on safe ground with Felsenstein. But complications set in as soon as the psychologist of the legitimate stage comes to the fore in the opera director. What did "really" happen that night? Felsentein begins to meditate, as though he were trying to interpret a Kafka novel. Donna Anna "is seized by hitherto unknown, overwhelming emotion which she cannot resist—the woman born to be Giovanni's partner is awakened and is stronger than Anna's conscience."[11] Here Felsenstein comes precariously close to Hoffmann's "voluptuous madness" by giving Anna's action an arbitrary interpretation which the director claims to have deduced "far more from the score than from the text."[12] He also asserts he is able to derive from the score that Donna Anna will not survive the year of mourning she and Don Ottavio had agreed upon. He senses that from the *larghetto* of the F-major aria with its "peculiar otherworldliness,. . . more a farewell than a pledge," and from the subsequent *allegretto moderato* with its "confident hope for release." Such fine nuances based upon an entirely subjective reaction to the music do not reach the ears of the listener, even if he did read Felsenstein's program notes in time before the lights went out.

The decors were by Reinhard Zimmermann, who stage left and stage right installed permanent, dark frames in wing positions, creating "alleys" for entries and exits. The polished wooden floor shone even in outdoor scenes. The backdrops were exchangeable. In fact, this was a modified Roller stage. It reminded the critic

Siegfried Melchinger of the Théâtre Italien stage, which Mozart had in mind when he wrote his opera. Within the framework of this nonillusionist stage Felsentstein invented some realistic touches as, for instance, in the Breughel scene of the peasant wedding or at Elvira's arrival in her coach. The recitative introducing Elvira's first entrance had always given directors the opportunity for what has been called "interpretation according to the action."[13] Elvira has now reached the goal of her journey from Burgos to Seville. A nineteenth-century director had here already discovered realistic possibilities: Elvira, dressed for traveling and accompanied by a maid and a porter, bargains in pantomime with the inn's *padrone* over lodgings. In Possart's production (Cuvilliés Theater, Munich, 1896) Donna Elvira arrived in a sedan chair. Actually, the audience doesn't care from what city, after how long a journey, or by what means of transportation the lady arrives in Seville. What the lady must bring to the stage is not her luggage but the voice required by her "*fuggi il traditor!*"

The early 1970s brought a series of new productions, remarkable for various reasons. In fact, 1973 could be called a veritable *Don Giovanni* year. It started in Munich; Berlin and Hamburg followed suit.

Director Günther Rennert, who was responsible for the Munich production, had tackled this opera several times. In 1971 he collaborated with the Czech designer Josef Svoboda in a Stuttgart production. At that time it was hardly conceivable that a director of Rennert's caliber would be satisfied with Svoboda's "decors." The latter built a basically black and red arrangement of platforms, ascending toward the back in strict graphic order. K. H. Ruppel described it as follows: "A geometric, right-angle-dominated scene whose individual sections meet with sharp edges. In some scenes framework constructs abut these sections. The frames accentuate even more the regular, circumscribed quality of the whole 'lay-out' and further emphasize the fact that it is a flawed construction."[14] Rennert had no choice but to mount his production against this background, more suitable for Handel than for

Mozart. Luckily, in Stuttgart there were singers on hand who overcame the visual fiasco.

For his Munich production (1973) Rennert engaged a congenial stage designer, Jürgen Rose, who created a baroque frame that took into account the demand for both space and intimacy. The graveyard scene was unquestionably the high point. Rennert once called *Don Giovanni* "incommensurable" and was conscious of the fact that in the end the key to the enjoyment of this opera was the personality of the singing protagonist. Ruggero Raimondi's Don determined the success of the Munich revival; he was acclaimed the "d'Andrade of our century."

When listening to the opera on records, removed from the influence of the staging concepts, I find no trace of decadence. Mozart's music is crystal clear. The so-called champagne aria (*Finchè han dal vino*) exudes uninhibited lust for life.

None of that could be felt in the Augsburg Stadttheater, when (1972) Peter Ebert produced the opera with the designer Hans-Ulrich Schmückle. Those two had but one central aim: "To show on the stage the crumbling, the corrosive aspects of Don Giovanni." The hallmark was Spanish baroque in a state of decadence. For Ebert the opera dealt with "the last twenty-four hours of a life in morbid dissolution. An exhausted organism, driven merely by the automatism of its reactions, can no longer register any success." The producers were proud of their handling of the finale: before the closing sextet all decorative elements disappeared. The ensemble sang in an empty, black-lined room under brightest lights. The Don Giovanni world had been swept away, although the six survivors were still enthralled by their recent experiences and drew the consequences from them.

Ebert had already mused over questions of detail. A year later Da Ponte was subjected to a veritable barrage of questions when Rudolf Noelte was stalking the opera in West Berlin.

Noelte, whose directorial reputation was established on the legitimate stage, approached his first operatic assignment (Deutsche Oper, West Berlin, 1973) with a high sense of responsibility.[15]

He began by analyzing the libretto for time hints. He tracked every *più tarde*, found significance in every mention of *sera* or *notte*, and came to the conclusion that the action of the opera took place within twelve hours, from late evening to sunrise. According to this, we are witnessing the last night in Don Giovanni's life. Because for Noelte the action is continuous and encompasses a time span of only twelve hours, the director became convinced—which does him proud as a rationalist—that it was impossible for the Commendatore to be buried already and have a monument. (A startling assertion for us Mozarteans, who, heretofore, had taken the graveyard scene at face value. We simply followed the libretto.) The Don recognized that the statue has the features of the Commendatore. *"Ehi! del Commendatore non è questa la statua?"* he asked Leporello, who then had to decipher the inscription which threatened the murderer with vengeance. This coincided with the conception of the naive viewer who did not rack his brains over questions of time but assumed that the Commendatore was buried at the proper time and received a suitable monument; that he talked to Don Giovanni and nodded his marble head in approval when Leporello invited him to supper. All this is for us part of the Don Giovanni myth.

But Noelte was not content with that. He hatched an absurd idea: the statue in the graveyard was not at all the last resting place of the Commendatore. Don Giovanni, still flushed from the wine he drank at the party, fell victim to a hallucination that made him believe he stood at the grave of the murdered man. Leporello was in horror of the graveyard; he trembled with fright and out of this fear invented the inscription. Only a rationalist could go so far as to apply such a devious psychological interpretation to a mythical motif. The "marble guest" is after all an inseparable part of the Don Giovanni saga, and no director can make an audience believe that we have here the figments of brains steamed up by wine or befuddled by fear. Hence it is not very astonishing that in Noelte's version the Commendatore did not appear in the end at all; we only heard his voice while Don Giovanni evidently died of a heart attack. Da Ponte would not have nodded his head to this anti-hocus-pocus; he would simply have shaken it. Surely, Mozart could not have invented any music to suit Noelte's graveyard scene. In the eighteenth century, Noelte's manner of dying on the stage was not acceptable; the burned-out hero was not yet stageworthy. Noelte permitted no buffo scenes. Everything turned into *dramma serio*. For the psychological penetration, as Noelte practiced it, he needed time. Not even the champagne aria was sung in *presto* tempo. If there was one phrase in the libretto that was decisive for the production, it was Don Giovanni's admission: "Today, everything goes wrong for me." (*"Oggi . . . vanno mal tutti quanti."*) This, by the way, is not a bad motto for Noelte's whole production, dominated by an autumnal mood, this time created by Jürgen Rose with a decadent fin-des-siècle baroque. Noelte moved all but one scene into the open air. Thus, the Don gave a garden party, to which there can be no objection; he also dined *al fresco* before he succumbed to his heart attack. Only once were we confronted with an interior: for the F-major aria of Donna Anna; a gloomy scene in which the lady assured her fiancé of her love as she stood next to the bier on which her dead father lay. Noelte also succeeded in distorting the final sextet. In the Berlin performances it did not have a liberating, purifying effect. Here nobody was happy about the death of him who had violated the world order; six people, all in distress, were still seeking a way out. Yet, the score, to which our untunable directors who can't read a single note like to refer, contains no disillusionment.

Four days after the Berlin production, the opera had a premiere in Hamburg. Götz Friedrich sat in the producer's chair. Like his master Felsenstein, the docile disciple also tried to pry into the antecedents of the actual stage action. Friedrich, too, was sure that Giovanni had been more successful in his advances to Anna than the lady was later prepared to admit to Ottavio. How does Friedrich know that? He saw the Anna figure at her first appearance in the following way: "Because at the decisive moment she discovered that it had not been Ottavio, she wants to know who had aroused in her expectations such as no other man had hitherto been able to awaken."[16] We thought, until now, that everything went wrong for Giovanni that day. We are, it seems, in error. Friedrich's depth psychology does not jibe with Anna's "*scellerato*" and "*traditore*," or her call for "*gente! servi!*" A woman in whom "hitherto unknown feelings" have been stirred up is unlikely to call for servants.

Not only is Friedrich a Felsenstein disciple, but he also knows his Bert Brecht and in the second act discovers "anti-Aristotelian" dramatic material. He noticed in the opera elements of a didactic play for people "who want to determine esthetically what constitutes a crime, and what does not, how it should be judged, how to expiate for it." In the case of Friedrich, we did not anticipate any "rebellious aspects" (even if dragged in by the hair) or "social determinism." He pointed out that Giovanni and Ottavio were fellow members of an aristocratic order presided over by the Commendatore (who cares?); that the hero, however, got sick and tired of the established social order and therefore sought self-realization in asocial behavior. Masetto and the other peasants were viewed through the eyes of Goya; the revolutionary flame, fed by storm and stress, still burned in them.

When Friedrich did not turn doctrinaire, he delivered good *dramma giocoso*. He whipped the action into *allegro* tempo, produced at times theater that broke the shackles of convention and did not hesitate to let Leporello give Giovanni a massage. For all these goings-on the old-fashioned wing-and-border stage, resuscitated by Toni Businger, was eminently suitable. Is some future Giovanni going to sing the champagne aria in the sauna?

We close the chapter with a few briefly noted perversions.

Whoever felt the need to see a brutal Don Giovanni had to make a pilgrimage to Kassel (1965), where the opera, instead of starting with a duel between Spanish grandees, began with an assassination. Leporello was caught up in the duel; he diverted the Commendatore's attention from Giovanni, who then had the opportunity to stab the Commendatore in the back. From here on we have lost all respect for the "hero" as well as for the director, Christoph von Dohnanyi.

Gian Carlo Menotti's production in Spoleto (1967) was under the spell of the sculptures by Henry Moore, who was responsible for the alienating decors. This resulted in a rather gloomy *Don Giovanni*. To be sure, the Don was the owner of a Moore statue, a sort of status symbol. The Commendatore also owned a statue, but was not quite certain where to put it. Additional Moore motifs were shown by projection and hence didn't cost anything. All this amounted to nothing more than an anachronistic fiasco. The ball scene became an antifestivity, where musicians with grotesquely distorted faces, that could have been painted by Hieronymus Bosch, played on fake instruments from which no sound issued. Giovanni, who shortly before his demise enjoyed a very realistic pheasant, was not so selective when it came to music: he accompanied his serenade not on a mandolin but on—a tin sieve. This was obviously in tune with his black leather outfit. Thus variety was provided, and the snobs who congregated at the festival had the satisfaction of seeing Mozart done differently for once—as a nightmare.

In Frankfurt (1969), too, Giovanni was divested of his demoniac nature. Ulrich Brecht (related to B. B. in spirit only) "demonstrated" his demythologized fable on a wooden podium with wing alleys, designed by Ekkehard Grübler. The dramatic character of the opera was stressed, the illusionary aspects were downplayed. The descent into hell was left out; the ghost simply dragged the debauchee offstage. This is one more solution to a scenic problem producers sought over the years to master with the help of smoke, Bengal lights, devils' masks, and simple exits through trapdoors.

Václav Kašlik attended to the Prague *Don Giovanni* of 1969. Josef Svoboda created the scenic frame, and it was a permanent one; painted decors were outlawed. The director had the absurd idea of extending the boxes of the auditorium onto the stage, including the two proscenium boxes in the play as well. There was no localized house of the Commendatore, no inn for Elvira; there were only boxes and more boxes, even in the cemetery. Kašlik's box circus was one more gimmick under which Mozart's music languished. Especially in Prague one might have expected a certain sense of responsibility for *Don Giovanni*. But there the world premiere of 1787 had long been forgotten.

In Cologne (1971) a production directed by Jean-Pierre Ponnelle was remarkable for the gags nobody had thought of before. Thus, Leporello always lugged with him the catalogue of Giovanni's conquests, from the first scene to the last. After all, something worth recording might happen even in the final moment. To indicate that there was some sort of activity in Anna's bedroom, silhouettes were projected on a palace window. When Anna acquainted us with her fiancé, she appeared on the arm of an elderly gentleman who in the course of the opera more and more resembled her father. A father complex?

In 1972 the New York City Opera presented a new *Don Giovanni*. Frank Corsaro furnished the directing ideas. He once assured us that he always "scrutinized" any libretto on which he had to work.[17] In that process he made perplexing discoveries never made before. For instance, he tried to convince us that Puccini's Mimi is basically a bitch, that Gounod's Marguerite had no claim on heaven but should have ended at the gallows, and that Violetta is no *traviata* but a downright whore. For Don Giovanni, Corsaro also had new insights: his Don is a whoremonger who never appears without some tart. With Zerline, who is well on her way to becoming a hooker, the Don rolls in the hay. (It was Hofmannsthal's Ochs von Lerchenau who praised the delights of bedding in the hay.) Furthermore, one cannot blame Zerline too much for her complaisance: she is not engaged to the robust peasant Masetto, as we all know him, but to a bespectacled schoolteacher type. Corsaro's Seville has an aura that reminds us of Hamburg's Reeperbahn (a disreputable amusement district), and it is not unexpected that the Don will spend his afterlife in a hellish bordello, if there is any credence to be given to the significance of the red lights.

In 1973 Covent Garden staged a new *Don Giovanni*. This time John Copley had the "ideas," and Stefano Lazaridis designed the abstract decors. When the audience entered the auditorium, the absence of a house curtain was noted. Even the prompter's box had been removed. Leporello was already on stage, hiding his identity under a cloak. Spain was also in hiding—no trace of it. Instead, a tangle of meaningless steel rods as background for the murder. What the scenery lacked in atmosphere was compensated for by the excessively rich baroque costumes under whose weight the singers had a hard time breathing. There were boos, and not without justification.

Whoever might have wished to enjoy an incapacitated Casanova should have been satisfied with Bohumil Herlischka's Duisburg production (1974). Here a sickly imagination was in charge and created a pestilential atmosphere. This Giovanni does not get drunk on champagne, not even on ordinary wine. He must have quaffed from the polluted waters of the nearby Rhine.

In 1977 Salzburg was again treated to a new *Don Giovanni*. Jean-Pierre Ponnelle functioned as both director and designer. As mentioned above, he had produced the opera in Cologne as early as 1971. Two years later we endured Rudolf Noelte's iconoclasm. His notions left their traces also in Ponnelle's Salzburg mise-en-scène. Once again darkness dominated Spain. No hint of a *dramma giocoso*. Karl Böhm, too, discovered the dark coloration of the music. The Don was no longer in his prime and was therefore a rebel and anarchist rather than a skirt chaser, who like Noeltes hero succumbed to a heart attack. Ponnelle had intimate, more reflective scenes sung in front of an interim curtain. This alternating between a deep and a shallow stage is essentially a stylistic element of the eighteenth century. When the entire stage was used, it was dominated by a sizable crucifix. Leporello had to drag a folio volume around, probably because he describes his master's list of sins to Elvira as "*non piccolo libro.*"

Demon, arch-seducer, sensualist, debauchee, Casanova, country squire, old lecher, anarchist, joie de vivre personified, taboo violator, amoralist, vagabond, cavalier—Don Giovanni appeared in all these guises, hardly to be recognized any more as an archetype, as though he wanted to shroud his identity beyond the first scene. The directors had a virtually endless choice in their often desperate and meaningless efforts to wrest from the music something Mozart steadfastly refuses to hand over.

Così fan tutte

We are in the realm of opera buffa. E. T. A. Hoffmann saw its essence in the "entering of the fantastic into ordinary life, and the resulting contradictions." He found the much maligned Da Ponte text "truly operatic," and undeserving of the contempt with which it was treated. In Mozart's "magnificent" music he heard the "expression of delightful irony" and of "the comical in all its nuances."

Beethoven had found the subject of the opera repulsive. For him, it could never become a source for music. He preferred to sing a paean to wifely fidelity. The prelude (act 1, scene 1) immediately aroused the displeasure of the composer of *Fidelio*. Two young officers, Ferrando and Guglielmo, raved about the faithfulness of their brides, the sisters Dorabella and Fiordiligi. A cynical older friend, Don Alfonso, tried to cure them of their naiveté: female faith is like the phoenix; everybody talks about that bird but no one has ever seen it. The bridegrooms were ready to defend the honor of their fiancées with the sword, but Don Alfonso suggested a less gory solution. Provided the two hotheads were willing to submit to a bet, he was ready to demonstrate the fickleness of females. The ensuing action proved Don Alfonso right, and the four young people became wiser in the "*scola degli amanti*." They ended by agreeing with Don Alfonso: *Così fan tutte*. Fiordiligi and Dorabella were no exceptions, and the search for the phoenix continued. Mozart had known all that from bittersweet experience, long before Da Ponte dared here to undermine a bourgeois tabu.

Legend has it that the Viennese *chronique scandaleuse* actually recorded such a bet, that Emperor Joseph II had got wind of it and that he had ordered Da Ponte to write a libretto for Mozart on this very theme. Was the great emperor of the Enlightenment trying to enlighten the lovers as well? In any case, *Così* was a command opera for which the composer received two hundred sorely needed ducats, although they did not cover all his debts. The opera had its premiere in 1790 in the Court Theater. One of the courtiers found "*la musique de Mozart charmante et le sujet assez amusant.*"[3] Whether the emperor attended the performance can not be ascertained. In any case, he died a few weeks later, and the performances were interrupted by justified national mourning. Actually *Così* did not recover from this semiofficial shock for a century. Already in 1792 a critic complained in Berlin: "The present-day *Singspiel* is the most inane stuff in the world." This remained, Hoffmann excepted, pretty much the consensus of the nineteenth century which mistreated this opera. The original Italian version barely survived the death of Mozart. Translations and arrangements began only a year later, and were by no means limited to the German language. Jules Barbier and Michel Carré, the librettists of Gounods' *Faust*, attempted in 1863 to base the opera on a French text derived from *Love's Labour's Lost*; this adaptation was staged unsuccessfully under the title of *Les peines d'amour perdues*. London saw a version called *Tit for Tat* (1828).

Did our century meet the test? Several attempts to decipher Mozart's esoteric score shall be discussed here.

Let us begin with the preludial first scene. Da Ponte had stipulated a Neapolitan café as the setting for the bet. A folding screen, a little table, three chairs, and three singers was all he needed. After all, it was his aim (and he knew his business) to make the conditions of the bet very clear. The surroundings were to remain abstract. But opera directors, especially when they come from the legitimate stage, have a *horror vacui*. They constantly strive to "enliven" the scene, to "create" atmosphere, to "motivate." Three cases from the recent past may serve as examples of how the prelude fared at the hands of our directors.

At the Glyndebourne Festival the scene was played in a pub, in the early morning hours, after the trio had caroused all night. The candles had almost burned down. The taproom boy had long been asleep on the floor. Carl Ebert was directing. This was his motivation: only in a state of inebriation could the three drinking companions have made a bet that questioned the faithfulness of women.

In Hamburg (1975), Götz Friedrich had a different brainstorm: he moved the bet backstage of a provincial theater that teemed with extras. These were drawn into the play by Don Alfonso and helped to carry out the masquerade when they reappeared in act 1, scene 5 as the soldiers' chorus. The two *amantis'* costumes "in the Turkish manner" came from the theater wardrobe. Farfetched and cumbersome premises for lilting music!

The prelude fared even worse in Strasbourg, where Werner Düggelin had the three gentlemen play cards in an establishment that closely suggested a brothel, since seminude ladies offered for sale not only spirits but quite obviously their physical charms as well. No wonder then that the two lovers could not lay claim to our sympathies since the opera began on the theme: *Così fan tutti*. The center of gravity was shifted. What was supposed to have been graceful and light late rococo became cheerless and clumsy. The ironic treatment with which Mozart and Da Ponte dealt with the "case," the artful texture of erotic confusions, was destroyed from the outset. What followed under Düggelin's direction could only be a miserable farce.

Götz Friedrich, by the way, should not be judged by his work in Hamburg but rather on his stage direction at the East Berlin Komische Oper (1962). There Friedrich directed with a stopwatch

33

in hand. Even the audience was not spared the time: above the proscenium was a baroque timepiece that continuously informed the public of the actual hour of the stage action. The action began at 3:00 A.M., and the masquerade ended at 9:30 P.M. the next evening. Could anyone possibly have been interested in chronometry while listening to Mozart's music? But let us forget the ticking of the clock. Friedrich's basic concept demands our attention. In his preparations he proceeded so methodically that Stanislavsky, who found it necessary to invent a "biography" for Rodrigo in *Othello*, would have beamed with joy. Friedrich began by researching the prehistory of the action. It turned out that the mother of the two sisters had died while giving birth to the younger. (Da Ponte must have forgotten that.) Since the father was a "natural scientist and globe-trotter," and therefore rarely at home, the semiorphans were dependent on the hired help. This information deserves a verbatim quote: "The children are more dependent on each other and on the housekeepers. Because they are very obstreperous, the latter change frequently. Above all, it was the older, bluestocking governesses who indignantly quit until a very young person, who also had a will of her own, appeared: Despina."[3] Amazing how much a director knows! Is it possible that we overlooked all that in the libretto? Let's check: not a trace about a globe-trotting father nor a bluestocking governess. Despina? All we see is a figure that came to Mozart's ken as a legacy from the commedia dell'arte, just as she later entered Strauss's artistic realm in the charming guise of Zerbinetta.

In his promptbook, Friedrich made observations on the individual characters. All six of them. Once more he exceeds by far what is necessary for the opera audience to know and what they can learn from the libretto. He opens the text as if it had seven seals. Examples: Because Fiordiligi had a father who was interested in the exotic, she took special interest in the costume of the Albanians (or Turks). Dorabella, who after all had the same father, did not inherit that interest in the exotic. She was "simply ripe like a magnificent apple," ready for picking. But genes are mandatory: hence she inherited something, namely, Daddy's "practical sense." We learn further details which we did not know before and which, now that we know them, we would like to forget. Such as, that Guglielmo was the "third son of landed gentry," while Ferrando was able to pursue an officer's career "thanks to the thrift of his parents." To all of this the unfortunate singers in East Berlin had to convey emotions, bound to the music of Mozart, without the help of Da Ponte. It is surprising that there are still so many singers craving an operatic career.

But we still haven't arrived at Friedrich's actual directing concept. It once more concerns the question of morality: first feudal, then middle-class morality has enslaved women, and Friedrich sees in this opera the first signs of a "social Utopia," a view toward a future of a "humanist world of freedom," in which the idea of faithfulness is no longer restricted by bourgeois morality. This superimposed ideological content close to Ibsen and Wedekind seems to me to be too heavy a freight for this opera to carry. Friedrich himself warns against extending social criticism to the characters of the women, whose feelings at certain moments are by no means expressed ironically in the score. Since Friedrich is programmed through his Weltanschauung to challenge the solid citizen, his attitude in this case must be accused of ambiguity if not ambidexterity.

Be that as it may, Friedrich showed no understanding of the directing concept that prevailed in the production of O. F. Schuh. Schuh's could be described as a chessboard concept, a geometric play in which the dramatis personae perform an amatory round dance. The Redoutensaal, the ballroom of the Vienna Hofburg (1943), suited such a solution: a puppetlike stylization which completely waived all local color and found sufficient decor in a couple of folding screens. Schuh was aware of the fact that at one point the geometry was disturbed and gave way to a "confusion of feelings" when Fiordiligi, in her great second-act aria (*"Per pietà"*), strove to return to her true self while accusing herself of having been possessed by *"smania, affano, leggerezza, perfidia e tradimento."* Here the marionette play ended. The strictly defined rules of the game temporarily yielded to confusion, to be resolved symmetrically at last into a Verdian *"Tutto in mondo è burla."*

Misdirection

Later (1953) Schuh's "spiritualized" idea of directing became the subject of debate during the Salzburg festival. In the arcade-lined court of the Residenz, once more atmosphere was omitted. "Decor" by Caspar Neher. Not even the light coming from six Venetian crystal chandeliers changed in the course of the evening. The singers were guided choreographically on an almost empty podium, a "*tréteau nue*" as Copeau would have called it. The Schuh-Neher production remained on the Salzburg calendar until the summer of 1959.

In 1969, Salzburg was ready once more for a new *Così* experiment. This time the responsibility lay with Jean-Pierre Ponnelle, to whom the direction, scenery, and costumes were entrusted. It was a bitter evening. Ponnelle fell into the snares of a cynicism which the music belies. We have here the prime example of a director whose intelligence easily outsmarts his modest musical sensibility. The emotional confusion of the sisters, of Fiordiligi especially, was genuine and articulated through Mozart's music; in this production it verged on parody. Don Alfonso assumed Mephistophelean traits. The usually sprightly maid Despina was changed into a procuress who must have plied her trade in the ghetto of Naples. What was presented that evening was not Molière's smile over his Alceste, but the misanthropy of a Wycherley, for which there is no musical equivalent. Ponnelle felt a fiendish pleasure in reminding us of the frailty of human relations.

During the festival season of 1969 in Munich things were much more cheerful. An Italian director, Franco Enriquez, was hired, who saw in *Così* not much more than another opera buffa in the Italian tradition and who, without intellectual qualms and with total lack of understanding of the score, transformed *Così* into an unbridled farce. Mozart sang "the breath of love" in many variations, but perhaps never with as much tender intensity as he saved for Ferrando's A-major aria "*Un aura amorosa.*" In Cuvilliés's rococo theater the aria was addressed to a Guglielmo who— lolled about on the floor. Ponnelle had interpreted the opera in a manner subtly defamatory; Enriquez went to the other extreme, into the shallow farcical. The audience waited for the man who would bring matters into balance at last.

In any event, by 1972, in Salzburg the need was felt for a *Così* with faith in the score. Günther Rennert was engaged to evoke the spirit of the Mozart world. After several trials in other cities, Rennert succeeded in creating a "model" for *Così* that remained in the Salzburg repertory for six festival summers. Schuh had directed the opera "with love for geometry" (Max Frisch) as a puppet play. The puppets were manipulated by the director and his house manager, Don Alfonso, on invisible wires. In contrast to Schuh, Rennert relaxed the play again. He directed the opera as a comedy of character in the manner of Molière. He did not overlook the typical in Da Ponte's figures, but neither did he fail to hear the human qualities that exuded from the music. Ita Maximovna's decor was the ideal complement to the directing concept. A few fishing nets, and we were in a harbor. Naples? Certainly, for there was Vesuvius with its little smoke cloud drawn with a few chalk lines on a blue background. A couple of door frames and we were in a villa. We didn't even miss the walls. In the garden stood a pavilion, as if made of Chinese porcelain. A few pieces of furniture on the oval platform underscored the artificiality of the entire directing scheme. When the two sisters were sad, even the furniture appeared to mourn, a mourning that could not be portrayed more ironically nor more in the spirit of Mozart.

The true rediscoverer of this opera, by the way, was Richard Strauss. He had attended the Munich performance under Hermann Levy in 1910, and commented on it in a Vienna paper where he defined the "humorous-pathetic, parodistic-sentimental" style of the opera.[4] In 1920 he gave musical expression to his admiration for *Così* in the Vienna Staatsoper. The *Rosenkavalier* master of the sung parlando knew how to appreciate Mozart's recitatives, neglected until then in favor of the arias. They awaited cultivation. Might an actor be of help here?

In the 1931–32 season, *Così* was under the directing care of the actor Gustav Gründgens at the Berlin Staatsoper unter den Linden. After ignoring *Così* for twenty-three years, the Metropolitan Opera ran a similar experiment with an actor-director in 1951. Rudolf Bing persuaded Alfred Lunt to embark upon the career of an opera director. Lunt, like Gründgens, was an expert at the conversational tone. *Così* could only profit from that, especially since this time the opera was sung in English (in the excellent translation by Ruth and Thomas Martin). Lunt, like Gründgens, had a great sense of style. What would be the basis for his directing concept? "Comedy of manners" was the magical formula, and it sparked immediately. During weeks of personal contact with the singers Lunt demonstrated rococo gestures; taught them minuet steps; pried their arms away from their chests. Nothing was left to spontaneous improvisation. The result was an enchanted evening in the superdimensional frame of the Old Met, which seemed to have been built for Caruso and Chaliapin and now had to do justice to Mozart's most intimate work in front of an audience of three thousand.

Lunt's *Così* started with a gag designed to put the audience in the right mood: at the end of the overture Lunt appeared as "a Servant" and turned on the footlights. The audience was thus transported into Munich's Cuvilliés Theater or even to Drottningholm. What Lunt achieved that evening he could not have mastered without the help of his designer, Rolf Gérard. His eight decors were more lush than those of Maximovna in Salzburg, with greater emphasis on local color while remaining within the framework of the rococo. "The scenery should look like china," said Gérard, and he succeeded. If the decor seemed to be made of porcelain, the costumes suggested spun sugar. Was there anything lacking that evening? Only Karl Böhm and the Vienna Philharmonic Orchestra.

In his Hamburg production, Götz Friedrich moved the bet in the prologue backstage of a theater, thereby creating a play within a play. This absurd idea was adopted in the Munich Nationaltheater by Gian Carlo Menotti in 1978. There again we were backstage. Don Alfonso appeard as the principal of a troupe of strolling players since he commanded stagehands, extras, and female singers who bustled about during the prologue and with their noise distracted from the essentials, namely the terms of the bet and the music. We were in the middle of opera buffa. The performance was peppered with *lazzi* which conflicted with the score in an irritating manner.

To round out the chapter, we remember an attempt to strike a bourgeois note at the finale of the second act, by a few changes in the libretto. In 1917, Emil Gerhäuser produced *Così* with Bernhard Pankok's decors in the small Stuttgart Hoftheater. He started with the idea that the two young officers, returned from the front for a short leave, discovered that they had made a mistake in the choice of their brides. In the course of the action they chose anew, and this time correctly. Ferrando (the tenor) is better suited to Fiordiligi (soprano), and Dorabella (mezzosoprano) finds in Guglielmo (baritone) her ideal husband. The "love" of the original partners was put to the test and turned out to be self-delusion. The maid Despina no longer masqueraded as justice of the peace; a real magistrate was brought in, and the marriage contract became legal. Cupid, no longer a rococo archer, finally pointed his arrows in the right directions, and there remained no obstacle to a double wedding ceremony. The material was divested of its frivolity and transposed into stodginess.

The Magic Flute

A great time was had by all at the Freihaustheater auf der Wieden after Emanuel Schikaneder established himself as its director. He satisfied the craving for entertainment of his unsophisticated audience with farces and fairy-tale *Singspiele*, some of which he wrote himself; in their production he stinted neither in decor nor in machinery.

One day, it was in the year 1791, he dreamed up another fantastic play, a checkered fairy-tale medley which included Egyptian Freemasons, a steadfast prince, an evil queen and her lovely daughter, a bird-man, a blackamoor, and a magic flute—another bit of fun for the simpler playgoers, this time with a humanitarian message as a slight bow to the moribund Age of Enlightenment. The official textbook was adorned with an engraving of Freemason emblems and a picture of Schikaneder as Papageno. Here we have the two worlds of a libretto which might very well have been put to music by a Paul Wranitzky or Wenzel Müller. In that case it would have passed unnoticed. But luckily, "poetry [became] the obedient daughter of music."[1]

Misdirection

In the course of its stage career, the libretto met repeatedly with lack of understanding. Time and again there were detractors who could not forgive Mozart's descent from Da Ponte's lofty heights to Schikaneder. Only in our century has the derogatory criticism of the text begun to subside, though Wolfgang Hildesheimer deals with it even in our days as an infantile fable.[2] Perhaps we simply overestimated Schikaneder when we loaded with meaning what was naively conceived.

Walter Felsenstein's production at the Komische Oper (East Berlin, 1954) was a case in point. The ideas which motivated the director were laid down in a report presented in 1958 by Felsenstein's assistant, Götz Friedrich, in a documentary volume.

There are obscure passages in the libretto which Felsenstein tried to clarify. He wanted Schikaneder to be "reasonable." Had anyone ever thought of what kind of wood the magic flute was made? Felsenstein submitted the libretto to a strict examination, and pointed out that Pamina revealed the secret of the flute's origin during a passage sung just before she went with Tamino to the ordeal by fire. "In a magic hour my father carved it from the very heart of a thousand-year-old oak while a storm was raging." This kind of information is invariably presented in librettos but ignored by the audience, no matter how distinctly it is articulated. Felsenstein, however, made sure we took notice of the flute's origin: he had his designer, Rudolf Heinrich, paint a show curtain in the style of a Chinese painting, showing Pamina's father as a wood-carver.[3]

Who had ever wondered about the identity of Pamina's father? Again it was left to Felsenstein to bring that good man from somewhere behind Szechwan nearer to us. Actually, the man did not appear, he was long dead. But the director saw to it that we should be aware of this background existence. The old king, it says in the book, was a friend of Sarastro, and when he felt his final hour approaching he gave the "sevenfold, all-consuming sun disk" into his friend's charge for he had no faith in his wife, the later Queen of the Night. He feared she might abuse that "sun disk." Since then Sarastro wears that "powerful sun disk" on his chest (according to the text). Mozart's contemporaries did not wrack their brains over that peculiar sun disk. If they had done so, they might have wondered why a wise man should wear something on his chest that was "all-consuming."

The royal widow wanted to acquire that symbol of power. To accomplish this, she needed the help of a sort of Parsifal, a "guileless fool by compassion wise," and Tamino appeared to be the proper instrument. This prince had a father who evidently was still alive, and for reasons unclear (the text says nothing about it) Felsenstein made him a partisan of the Queen. Friedrich, in his commentary, has further details to report concerning the relationship of Tamino's father with the nocturnal queen: "Although he had never seen her face-to-face, he worshipped her fabled beauty and the imagined glory of her appearance so much, that even for his adolescent son the name of the Queen of the Night became the essence of everything mysterious and beautiful." Here assumptions are carried too far. The text merely says that Tamino's father had often talked to his son about the queen.

Felsenstein's passion for genealogy reminds us of E. T. A. Hoffmann's parody in his "Strange Sufferings of a Theater Manager." There "the Gray One" tells, with "inventive irony," of an attempt to change the fairy tale into melodrama: the defunct husband of the Queen of the Night was declared to be the older brother of Sarastro, while Tamino's father was elevated to the role of younger brother. When Sarastro discovered that Pamina was brought up badly by her mother (she was forced to read Goethe's novels!), he, as her uncle, took custody of the girl. That makes Pamina Tamino's cousin, and Tamino no less than Serastro's nephew. Papageno, too, is made a member of the family. He is a natural son of the nocturnal queen, sired by the elusive—"Duke of Parrots"! Said Hoffmann's Gray One in conclusion: "You see, my good friend, how magnificently these relationships interact and thereby create the truly emotional elements of the subject matter."

He who does not trust the fairy tale or the Viennese sense of fun will also find a problem in Monostatos. Here, too, Felsenstein thought long and hard. He wanted to "liberate" the black man

from buffo by elevating him to a "Nubian prince" who had served
Sarastro long and faithfully. However, his creeping up on Pamina
in the garden is not exactly princely behavior. No matter what ex-
cuse Felsenstein makes for him, if the Queen had not been there
in time with her "Away!" the "noble" Moor would have tried to
rape the girl. The revaluation of the Moor is a hopeless attempt
since Felsenstein could not do away with the bastinado which is in
the score.

His inquiries continue.

Let us turn to the initiated. Consensus has it that Schikaneder
was thinking of some lodge in Egyptian guise. Since under Leo-
pold II the Josephine spring had turned into a dreary, reactionary
late fall, such a disguise was advisable. The initiates were no doubt
proponents of humanity, fraternity, and equality. They could have
signed the Helsinki Pact and would have abided by it. But Felsenstein again went too far when he spoke of the order's "democratic
structure" and credited its members with the following: "The initiates sent out by the order heal pestilences, dam floods, build ca-
nals, create arable land, build streets and settlements." Which
made them a sort of Peace Corps. From the dialogue between the
Speaker and Sarastro, Felsenstein again drew unwarranted conclusions. He talked about "tension" within the order between the conservative "supreme council" and the progressive Sarastro. An un-
prejudiced reading of the text shows that the reservations against
Tamino's admission were promptly overcome and that the initiated
were quick to blow their horns of consent. When Richard Mayr
sang Sarastro in Vienna or Salzburg with the softest, fullest, most
sensitive basso profundo, there was no "tension" but only sweet
harmony. Since we no longer have singers of such quality—Kipnis
and Weber were the last ones—the directors feed our Sarastros
ideological fare to make up for the missing low F.

Felsenstein did not know what to do with the Freemasonry.
Quite evidently, he was unsympathetic to it. He considered its
ideas a Viennese fad of the time, and found in the work "less Freemasonry than quite simply revolutionary undertones." He pointed
to the fact that the order refused to accept a prince. We are sup-

posed not to take too seriously what Schikaneder wrote. After all, we are no longer guests at Beaumarchais's. Here Felsenstein might have echoed Ernst Bloch, who also whittled on the magic flute in one of his hours spent with the Muses, and who pointed out that, at the time when the libretto originated, "there was revolution in the air."[4]

That brings us to the choral part of the two finales. "The people" played a decisive role in Felsenstein's direction. They greeted Sarastro on his return from a (rather feudal) hunt; they witnessed the trials by fire and water and finally embraced Sarastro enthusiastically, after the members of the chorus emerged from the orchestra pit into the now illuminated auditorium. General fraternal rejoicing!

Sarastro still prayed to Isis and Osiris, but an Egyptologist could have taken no pleasure in Heinrich's setting. The designer gave the delicate fairy-tale play a rather heavy baroque frame that extended into the auditorium by masking the proscenium with a triple-tiered temple wall. The designer reasoned: *The Magic Flute* is indebted to the baroque theater. The flexible side scenes that could enlarge or narrow the stage area, displayed Far Eastern designs. Persian and Indian motifs were mixed in the costumes. Papageno lost his feather garment; he had become more "human" and only wore a bird mask. Sarastro and his people donned monastic garb of emphatic simplicity. Monostatos remained the black in a white society but he no longer appeared comical, rather was of princely stamp. The bastinado to which he was supposed to have been subjected (an exotic joke for the Viennese) could hardly be reconciled with Felsenstein's general concept.

Felsenstein, a native Austrian, knew of course how to produce magic theater, and in this respect he remained faithful to the exigencies of the libretto. He even outdid Schikaneder: during Papageno's glockenspiel performance he "materialized" in pantomime the sexual desires of that nature boy by conjuring up three half-naked women. Tamino's flute became imbued with a truly magic character: it played "by itself," after the prince had merely put it to his lips. After the trial by fire the lovers appeared in singed garments and with sooty faces. A violation of the artistic limits, a stylistic faux pas. The spiritual content of the trial loses out when it is debased to a circus act. We are tuned to believe that the melody of the flute insures the lovers against fire damage.

Four weeks after the premiere, an East Berlin daily published an essay by Arnold Zweig, in which the novelist ridiculed all pre-Felsenstein productions of the opera, because they had shown a bearded Sarastro and "seminarists" in white cassocks, but had failed to stress "the pursuit of happiness by the working people" as represented by Papageno. Zweig ended his article with a vision: a delegation from the German Democratic Republic approaches the pauper's grave of Mozart to express their thanks. They assure the mortal remains of the composer that the "injustice" done to his opera so far had been redressed at last by the "democratic Berlin."[5]

The Egyptian pomp of the court theater, today an easy subject of scorn on both continents, did not impair the pleasure of the Mozart fans for over a century; even if they could not penetrate "the heavy, dark veil of the allegory," as one critic wrote only a year after Mozart's death,[6] they nevertheless surmised the message proclaimed by two lodge brothers, without having the feeling that they were exposed to a *Lehrstück*.

In Vienna (Hofoper, 1906) Gustav Mahler still celebrated the mysteries with fairy-tale piety and absolute trust in the score. He was burdened with the designs which Josef Hoffmann, the "historical landscape artist," had created in 1869 for the new Hofoper. Hoffmann was deeply immersed in Egypt. Mahler had modifications made by Alfred Roller, F. A. Rottonara, and Anton Brioschi. Obviously, this did not result in a uniform mis-en-scène.

The next quarter of a century saw decorative experiments without deep reflection on the spiritual content of the opera. "Fairy-tale mystery"—that was approximately the watchword for the directors. There followed attemps to do justice to it with the Relief Stage, then again with projections and shadow effects; expressionism also laid its claim, and finally cubism.

This brings us to the Kroll Opera (Berlin, 1929) where Otto Klemperer charged the Bauhaus architect Ewald Dülberg with the scenery and the directing. Dülberg created an abstract stage space that emanated icy cold, while the conductor saw to it that no warmth radiated from the music either. Fritz Krenn's Viennese Papageno was the only executor of Mozart's legacy. Schikaneder would have been ashamed of that production and might at best have found some pleasure in Dülberg's Chinese costumes; for those, however, he would have written an altogether different libretto.

In 1938 (Staatsoper, Berlin) the team of Gustav Gründgens, Herbert von Karajan, and Traugott Müller brought *The Magic Flute* closer to Mozart again. Although just then Hitler's henchmen were arresting Austrians who doubted the thousand-year duration of the *Ostmark*, there was great rejoicing over Mozart in Berlin. Gründgens had discovered the singspiel; Müller conjured onto the stage a fantastic arcadian landscape in the style of the Barbizon School; and young Karajan paid musical homage to his Salzburg compatriot.

Associations demand at this point that we recall some of the Salzburg attempts to make *The Magic Flute* palatable to a festival audience. The Old Festspielhaus was the first site where famous conductors presented "their" *Magic Flute:* Franz Schalk did it with subtlety; Bruno Walter, with warmth; Arturo Toscanini, con brio. Their influence on the decor was negligible. The artist who was first responsible for the visual aspects in Salzburg (1929, 1931, 1932), was Oskar Strnad, Austria's greatest genius in stage design since the days of Roller. He was confronted with a relatively shallow stage which forced him to build vertically. He constructed a white and gold frame around the stage, not always to the advantage of the scenery behind it.

The Salzburg Felsenreitschule with its intractable arcades hewn from the rocky well was twice pressed into the service of *The Magic Flute.* In 1949 with Furtwängler on the podium, Oskar Fritz Schuh as director, and Caspar Neher as stage designer. Then again, in 1955, with Georg Solti as conductor, Herbert Graf as director, and Oskar Kokoschka as stage designer. Mozart in the Felsenreitschule—an expression of disdain for the wing-and-border stage to which the work was indebted. It was the time when in England the "true" Shakespearean stage was discovered, and Continental producers were satisfied with a merely suggestive podium.

It was mere chance that the performance of 27 July 1949 was not rained out. Many rehearsals were held under umbrellas. Nevertheless, none of the singers got hoarse. A year earlier Gluck's *Orfeo* had passed the open-air stage test. For this occasion, Caspar Neher had designed a central gate with adjacent arcades. These architectonic elements were now also used for Mozart, although softened with golden festoons entwining the Gluck columns. The (belated) baroque was introduced with a gloriole of clouds and a gilded sun. Schuh attempted (not without effort) to keep "the whole thing light and airy." But a bit of solemnity also seemed in order, which was more successful than the airiness. When the vitality of one or the other singer came to the fore, primarily so in the Papageno of Erich Kunz, we were in the magic sphere of the opera. The performers had no support in the decor and found themselves largely condemned to a static existence. In 1950, the production was repeated, and much was improved. Now the Queen of the Night appeared on top of the Mönchsberg while, simultaneously, the arcades filled with gray-veiled supernumeraries, evidently the train of the lunar sovereign.

In 1955, Oskar Kokoschka succeeded in bringing color to the rigid confines of the Rocky Riding School. He built a temple area with a tapering perspective. The architectonic elements showed strong coloration. The cobalt blue wall clashed with the orange architrave. The jolly painter had Indian yellow, carmine red, turquoise, green, purple, and pink in his paint pots.[7] Colored light lent additional symbolic value: from yellow to red for the Sarastro scenes; blue and purple for the realm of the nocturnal queen. The second finale was bathed in a sunrise.

In 1974, the Grosse Festspielhaus in Salzburg became the arena in which the battle between good and evil was fought. Von Karajan conducted, not exactly con amore. There had been tension between the maestro and the director, Giorgio Strehler, who had engaged the stage designer Luciano Damiani. The two Italians, confronted with a stage over ninety feet wide (Schikaneder had only a proscenium width of twenty-eight feet at his disposal), regressed into the eighteenth century, the great era of scenography. They thought they owed it to their illustrious technical predecessors to outdo the latters' baroque stage arts with present-day technical means. In this they succeeded. It all began as on the first day of creation: the stage was completely empty. The dinosaur which pursued Tamino had plenty of leeway. Eventually, a palm grove grew out of the earth. Rocks entered from the side. Later on, backdrops were lowered from the gridiron, and painted flats unfolded as soon as they touched the stage floor to give the illusion of three dimensions. Sarastro's temple emerged from a cloud gloriole of which even Giuseppe Galli-Bibiena would have been proud. The audience anticipated the next scene change with chill curiosity, and the perfection of the technical apparatus was duly admired. The stage floor was covered with silver foil, so we knew right away that we were to expect a frosty evening. Time and again we caught ourselves forgetting the music and the message over the visual feast. The audience's thoughts were preoccupied with technocracy rather than philanthropy. If there were such a thing as a malpractice insurance for artists, those responsible for the production would have stood in need of it.

When the Metropolitan Opera invited Chagall to design the decors for *The Magic Flute* (1967), Günther Rennert was faced with the task of making his directing concept prevail against Chagall's color orgy. The riot of colors started with the overture. Fantastically irrelevant surrealist figures gamboled in a Hasidic paradise on a show curtain in total contradiction to the chaste and precise music. One did not know what to close, one's eyes or one's ears— a discord prevailing the entire evening. Mozart's music could not overcome the obscene excrescences from Chagall's paint pots. Chagall had designed as if for a Diaghilev ballet with music by Rimsky-Korsakov.

In the 1970 Munich production, Rennert saw the opera in a different light. His scenic collaborator, Josef Svoboda, was not a famous painter but a technologist in charge of the secrets of lighting as Sarastro was in charge of the sun disk. "Decorations" were tabu this time; the stage designer considered them too static. He aimed at "kinetic" space, light-structures that would dynamically adapt to the action. New technical territory was opened through the use of the "stage laser"; with its aid Svoboda developed his "light designs," sometimes with startling effects. It was a sterile production, though, the "endgame" of the fairy tale.

There seems to be no dearth of Czech stage designers when a Mozart opera is to be produced in Western Europe. In 1967, Vladimir Nyllt was called from Prague to Cologne to collaborate with director Ladislav Stroš on *The Magic Flute*. In Cologne, too, the key word was "kinetic scenery." The audience was booked for a space trip and was no longer able to answer Tamino's question, "What *do* you call this region?"

But back to Munich, where *The Magic Flute* is the usual featured festival attraction. So it was in the year 1964. At that time Harry Buckwitz from Frankfurt was responsible for the directing, the Corsican Michel Raffaelli for the decors. The director had promised to bring to the stage "the poetry of the unobtrusive, of closeness to reality, of what is taken seriously." As soon as Buckwitz escaped the foggy thicket of the German language and had to make friends with the unequivocal dimensions of the Munich stage, a lot of things went wrong. No starry sky sparkled for the Queen of the Night; she was turned into a sort of witch, an earth spirit who sang her glittering coloraturas from a cloven tree trunk. Sarastro's palace resembled a miserable hermitage in which at best an anchorite could feel at home.

In 1966, a new production at the Munich festival. Director, Rudolf Hartmann; stage designer, Herbert Kern. The ambiance of the Cuvilliés Theater was both a help and a commitment. This time they came very close to Mozart. The Queen of the Night got her starry sky back, an impressionistic version of the classical Schinkel decor of 1815. The woods were once more magical without obtruding.

It hardly pays to pause for the Peter Hall production of the same year in Covent Garden. Although Hall had voiced the opinion that *The Magic Flute* was related to Shakespeare's *Tempest*, he and his designer John Bury decided to present the English public with nothing but another version of the traditional Christmas pantomime. Papageno—he was Harlequin, of course; Papageno—Columbine, what else? God bless John Rich! No position was taken as to the spiritual content of the libretto. One was satisfied with a machine play. Even today the English cannot agree as to which translation of the libretto is the worst.

In 1967, the "incommensurable" opera moved again into the Grosse Festspielhaus in Salzburg. On this evening, O. F. Schuh offered a new variation of the work. The accent rested on the Sarastro mystery. The Viennese folk comedy was swallowed up by the gigantic stage, although Herman Prey's Papageno received scenic support from plant life sprouting here and there from the stage floor. Sarastro and his followers fared better. Their world passed like a dream. Mozart's Freemasonic tunes received an unforgettable optical equivalent in the scenic visions of Teo Otto.

Yet one more adventure during our travel through the recent Mozart past: *The Magic Flute* in the Vienna Staatsoper (1974). Director: Joachim Herz, a disciple of Felsenstein; decors by Rudolf Heinrich. Herz was thoroughly familiar with the ideas of his late master. He, too, had no doubt as to the quality of the libretto. From Felsenstein Herz had borrowed the idea that Sarastro and the initiates must also undergo a spiritual evolution in the course of the action: they approach wisdom when they accept Pamina into their male world and when they drop their objections to a prince. On the other hand it cannot be overlooked that they will still keep slaves and believe in corporal punishment. "The people" played an important role in Vienna just as in the Komische Oper in East Berlin; they dominated both finales. The Queen of the Night was revaluated by Herz. He saw positive aspects in her character as well. After all, it was she who had presented the prince with the flute that would help him liberate Pamina. However, this is not the whole story. Herz overlooked that the Queen was not so much interested in the recovery of her daughter as in regaining the "sun disk." For her this symbol of power was what the ring is to Alberich. Only that made her pact with Monostatos and her intrusion into the temple understandable. And didn't she put the dagger for the murder of Sarastro in her daughter's hand? Sarastro informed the priests that it was the goal of the Queen of the Night to destroy the solid temple of the order. A moral revaluation of the Queen is contrary to the intentions of the librettist. Heinrich created an enchanted wood, a labyrinthine forest à la *Midsummer Night's Dream* in which the invaders had a hard time finding their way. The action took place in a fantastic Asia where Persian, Indian, and Japanese elements mingled.

Nowadays directors are fond of encouraging brawls in our opera houses. Boos are then received as if they were bouquets of roses. In Stuttgart (1978) once more a production was up for dissent. Hans Werner Henze, successful producer of his own operas, had the ambition to prove himself as a Mozart director, which meant to approach *The Magic Flute* with a new concept. Away with all the Egyptian rubbish and Far Eastern dross. Were not Mozart and Schikaneder children of the Josephian Enlightenment? Isn't this opera permeated with Josephian thoughts? What was nearer at hand than Sarastro's identification with Emperor Joseph II? Sarastro indeed appeared in Stuttgart in a long, black frock coat, tight short pants, knee stockings, and bag wig. His train of courtiers followed the imperial fashion. Pier Luigi Pizzi had chosen the interior court of a palace as permanent place of action (in fact, a nonplace) for the fairy-tale plot. Of course the colorful variety of Schikaneder's scene sequences resisted such visual poverty and rigidity, even when, from time to time, set pieces were brought up from beneath the stage. The Viennese singspiel was starving, which would have given pleasure to the imperial reformer, and Herr von Sonnenfels would have rubbed his hands with glee. But what is a *Magic Flute* without a snake? We had laughed before over stage snakes that tottered onto the boards on legs of extras; now the audience laughed at the absence of the snake. Had it missed its cue?

I had hardly made notes of the imperial alienation when the

news arrived of a new blow at *The Magic Flute*. It came from the Palais Garnier in Paris (1978), where director Horst Zankl and his designer Arik Brauer approached the work as psychoanalysts. Unsuspected psychic chasms were opened up as if it were the case of *Electra*, in order to demonstrate that Sarastro's realm was a fraud, where people were oppressed and all the talk about fraternity was nothing but talk. Just look at Sarastro's servants: were they not lunatics, fit for an asylum? Hence Zankl chained them together. He demoted Monostatos to a kind of Caliban. It was therefore not surprising that at the sound of Tamino's gentling flute ugly monsters appeared instead of friendly animals. This time the snake did not miss its entrance and was slaughtered so thoroughly that its blood flowed all over the boards. We have reached the nadir of Mozart productions.

The sufferings of this eternally young opera are not yet at an end. Further trials lie in the offing. A perfectly tuned flute would only be received with boos in our secularized world. Richard Wagner had pondered repeatedly over the feasibility of reproducing classical works, especially *The Magic Flute*. In his essay "The Audience in Time and Space" ("Das Publikum in Zeit und Raum") he spoke of the stamp of immortality on Mozart's operas, and he continued resignedly: "Immortality!—What a fateful consecrated gift! To what torments of existence is the dead soul of such a masterwork exposed when, through some modern theatrical medium, it is martyred back to life again for the pleasure of posterity."[8]

Fidelio

Leonore, Fidelio, these were the problem children of the composer. He had long wrestled with the material before he found the final form which would stand up musically and dramatically for over a century and a half.

The *Fidelio* of 1814 had a clear message: that humanitarianism would triumph in the end; that prayers are heard; that evil can be eradicated; that Schiller's "Ode to Joy" has been vindicated; that the personal commitment of a courageous woman sets aright again a world out of joint. In short, the German idealism had been set to music and had prevailed.

In our century, this credo began to be questioned, which led to nihilism and the defacement of this opera. Testimonies as to the discomfort elicited by an idealistic work will be noted in the following pages, when the quest for a new "relevance" will be discussed. The moral decay of Minister Fernando, who brings freedom to the captives, is symptomatic. Nowadays, we no longer know what to do with a deus ex machina; he is doomed to be suspect.

We shall meet with another sore spot: the prose dialogues, which are considered musty and philistine. To focus on just one objection, what singer could nowadays be expected to speak the following sentence with conviction: "I maintain that the union of two hearts that are attuned to each other is the source of true marital bliss"? Thus Leonore, to continue "with warmth," as the stage direction prescribes: "Oh, this bliss must be the greatest treasure on earth!" Here the directors discovered cracks in the *Fidelio* cosmos, which they tried to mend in various ways, mostly with deletions but also by more brutal means.

On the other hand, it must not be overlooked that the antiquated text was accepted as a challenge by some singers. Lotte Lehmann, an unforgettable Leonore, admitted in her memoirs: "I have always enjoyed speaking the dialogue and regret that it is now cut for the most part." She found the spoken word in this particular opera especially vital and powerful. As an example, she cited the prose dialogue placed between Rocco's gold aria and the trio. The various emotions experienced by Leonore during this dialogue were for Madame Lehmann a task for a great tragedienne. Leonore believed she was approaching her goal; she had received the permission of the jailer to accompany him to the nethermost dungeon; the circumstance that one of the political prisoners had been languishing for two years in a special keep made Leonore almost sure that he was her husband, who disappeared two years ago. Without this spoken section, the subsequent trio does not make sense. To be sure, the singers are supposed to speak their lines without pathos, and Lotte Lehmann admitted that she was not always successful in solving the problem.

Once she discussed the matter with Max Reinhardt, who proposed the following remedy: "He would have the whole dialogue stylized, almost without expression, more as a kind of melodious speech which flows out of the music and back into the music."[2] What Reinhardt had in mind seems to be a sort of recitative. We shall encounter other suggestions.

It is the miracle of this score that out of a middle-class singspiel emerges a hymn to humanity and liberty, a dichotomy which meant only embarrassment to our directors. They would have preferred to start right away with the prisoners.

Beethoven had taken great pains with Joseph Sonnleithner's translation of J. N. Bouilly's libretto. Only after the pedestrian G. F. Treitschke had made scenic and textual changes on the basis of the Breuning version did the final *Fidelio* (1814) crystalize out of *Leonore I* (1805) and *Leonore II* (1806).

But nothing seems to be permanent for our directors and conductors—often one and the same person. The question which overture is to be played (and where) causes sleepless nights for the conductors: the unproblematic one in E-major or the overwhelming one in C-major? It is hard to understand that even Mahler inserted the C-major overture after the prison scene. By its very nature, it should open the opera, as a musical anticipation of the dramatic action, just as the *Egmont* overture anticipates the stage action. It was not meant to be a concert piece nor a means to facilitate the stagehands' shifting of the scenery in time.

Mahler's Viennese *Fidelio* (1904) should engage us for a while. In retrospect it might be said that the production was uncomplicated because it stuck to libretto and score. Alfred Roller's decors would satisfy esthetically even today. Rocco's habitat with flowers and sunshine had the intimacy that the music suggested. Philistine? Certainly. But it is the crucial point, that in the middle of this philistine milieu stood a heroic woman, disguised as a man, fortunately accepted by everyone for what she seemed to be, solely faithful to her mission of saving her husband.

Roller had taken care of everything. The prison was a fantastic, foreboding structure, from which the captives crept into the yard through semicircular holes. A green tree projecting over the prison wall had turned into a symbol of the freedom for which they yearned. A velvety, damp, dripping night pervaded the subterranean dungeon. It seemed hewn into the wet, smooth rock that glistened like anthracite. For the second finale, Roller immersed the bastion in golden sunlight with a smiling Spanish landscape in the background, the perfect scenic equivalent of the C-major finale.[3]

Misdirection

In 1904 the world appeared sound. To be sure, unrest was sizzling in the Balkans. But *l'amour conjugal* retained its validity despite Arthur Schnitzler, and the opera did not show any fissures. The work was accepted "naively" in Schiller's sense, no questions asked.

The first World War was to destroy this arcadian dream. Otto Klemperer's *Fidelio* (Krolloper, Berlin, 1927) is symptomatic. Adolf Weissmann sensed what was in the air when he reviewed the production: "What was prepared for weeks and months is a monomaniacal exaggeration of new production principles, a manifestation of dogmatism . . . a, one might say, spectacular one-sidedness, which could have grave consequences for the opera."[4] Klemperer not only conducted, he also directed. Ewald Dülberg was the stage designer. He had little sympathy for Rocco's lower-middle-class interior: a whitewashed, angular room, almost without furniture. There still was a table with laundry on it. The prison yard, a cubist piece of architecture whose rectangular building blocks could have brought no joy to the prisoners, especially since as inmates they were deprived of all individuality and had to move in lockstep like robots, a drill session in front of an isometric background. The ultimate of vocal intensity was demanded of the soloists, who also were led like marionettes. Bauhaus sterility dominated everywhere.

The year prior to the Kroll experiment, Arthur Maria Rabenalt and his stage designer, Wilhelm Reinking, had wrestled with *Fidelio* in Würzburg.[5] The production bore the stamp of the "New Functionalism Style." There was no lower-middle-class gemütlichkeit in Rocco's room. The prison yard showed naked concrete walls and steel constructions: a modern penitentiary. "As unromantic as Beethoven's music," the director declared. For the finale, a "scenic abstraction" to set off a "hymn, sung as if in a concert hall": prison ruins as a basis for a new order. In the costuming, too, every allusion to a historical past was avoided. *Fidelio* was presented here as a timeless scenic cantata. "The dialogue must be factual, unromantic, unsentimental, and terse" (Rabenalt). Marzelline was no soubrette; Jaquino no buffo. Not only Leonore, but these secondary characters as well, were bursting with "psychic tension." They, too, were "under heavy internal pressure." The prisoners moved like circus horses in the ring. They could not sing bel canto but had to be satisfied with a "single, thin ray of sunshine," while still retaining the text: "Farewell, warm sunlight. . . ."

I am beginning to wonder about these prisoners. Are they supposed to crawl out of holes, more like animals than men, and hardly able to stand straight? Or should they be clothed decently and still march with dignity in lockstep? Should they wear striped prison garb and stand in groups, covered by the armed guards? Are we in a more or less humane penal institution or in a concentration camp? In the forecourt of hell, perhaps? How can the hymn to the sunlight be made optically viable? Several solutions will be forced upon us. After World War II, the shadows of Auschwitz also fell on *Fidelio*. The temptation to hang Himmler's portrait in the operatic prison was by no means unthinkable. Postwar directors reacted skeptically to Beethoven's theodicy, if they did not reject it completely. The idealism of the old libretto seemed to have crumbled, as directors reached out for "new relevance."

The original dialogues of the opera were banned as nonsensical. Should they be modernized, or unmercifully eradicated and the musical numbers then bridged in some other way? Perhaps even Klemperer had considered the dialogues inadquate, but he still left them intact. It remained for Wieland Wagner to exorcise them in his Stuttgart production (1954). To render the plot intelligible, Wieland had to engage a "Speaker" who, illuminated by a spotlight, explained the course of events as if he were Milton Cross. One had the feeling that Wieland was embarrassed by the simplistic rescue story which Beethoven had deigned to set to music. Short shrift was made of the singspiel idyll: it was too bourgeois for Wieland's taste. His stage set, consisting mostly of five steel gratings as walls on the periphery of an acting circle, was anything but bourgeois. The gratings contracted or expanded the abstract "space." Here every character was "imprisoned." "Constraint" was all-pervasive. Everybody lived in "tension." The direction was still rooted in late German expressionism. The music was also subject to questionable experiments. The evening began with the second Leonore overture. Marzelline's aria preceded the duet. The E-flat major trio was borrowed from *Leonore I*. The second finale sounded static like an oratory, a paean to joy sung in a dreary wasteland. Wagner looked upon the actors as almost baroque types: Florestan, the hero of liberty; Pizarro, nothing but a tyrant; the Minister, an apostle of humanism; Rocco, greed personified; Leonore, conjugal love.

For his Brussels production Wieland changed his concept, perhaps because the Stuttgart production had met with resistance when it was brought to Paris. There was no "Speaker" in Brussels. Replacing him were somewhat rejuvenated, short dialogues with less emphasis on the oratorial aspects. But Wieland's idea of a "Speaker" continues to lurk about the German stages.

Ulrich Melchinger produced *Fidelio* in Kassel (1968). The Sonnleithner-Treitschke dialogue was unacceptable. Since nobody could be found who was willing to write a new prose script, someone came up with the startling idea of linking the musical numbers with prose and poetry of such writers as Brecht, Nelly Sachs, and Apollinaire. The duet between Marzelline and Jaquino was deleted; it was "too cute." The gold aria was also sacrificed, although it characterized so well the Rocco who, later on, had no objection to accepting Pizarro's bribe. Why the singers who played Rocco and Jaquino also had to sing the solo parts of the prisoners remains a mystery. The entire directional concept borrowed from Wieland Wagner remained meaningless: a scenic oratorio. The chorus occupied a stair scaffolding on the bare stage, while the principals, in civilian clothes, "acted" or, rather, "demonstrated" in the Brechtian vein on the main playing area. Above the stage, a human face repeated in a series of photomontages formed a border. The idea for this frieze might have been derived from Andy Warhol. Florestan's arms were immobilized by an ingenious traction device. Suitable music should have been commissioned from Dallapiccola.

In Wuppertal (1969) the connecting "Speaker" was revived.

Moreover, tape recordings of "interior monologues" of the characters involved were delivered not by the singers but by some actors' voices. This time, poor Florestan suffered in some sort of stocks, whose "ruff" collar must have been quite uncomfortable for the tenor. But the real shock for the audience came at the end. After the prison scene the opera came to a standstill. The lights were turned on in the auditorium; the C-major overture was played. Then the "Speakers" appeared and announced to the befuddled listeners that, from now on, they would have to cope with a cantata performance in a concert hall, and that the singers would appear in civilian clothes. The Minister's act of mercy, the "Speaker" claimed, was nothing but a hoax. Who could believe, as director Kurt Horres tersely put it, in "humanitarianism as a gift from a benevolent regime?" Down with the old clichés! To provoke reflection was the aim. The concern was with a "dramaturgy of upset." The expectations of the audience were to be "upset" through vigorous manipulation (*Umfunktionieren*), and the bewildered subscribers staggered out of what had become a politicized concert hall.

Watch out! Don Fernando is about to be transformed into a villain. In Magdeburg (1969), he was the target of skepticism. The director, C. R. Schau, cautioned the audience against the Minister, whose behavior was nothing but a "liberalistic maneuver of deception." Just look! He even had a priest in his retinue, and there was praying and kneeling! He commuted only the sentences of selected political prisoners in order to appease the rebellious crowd. Leonore's act of deliverance just suited his purpose. He praised her deed and even brandished a dirty tricolor. At the same time he came to an understanding with Pizarro, on whose advice the soldiers' guns must separate the prisoners from the people. The reactionaries obviously had the upper hand again. Schau wanted to demonstrate how difficult the battle for liberation is for humanity. He also wished to emphasize that the ideals of classical humanism can only be realized in a socialist society. "Let brother seek his brothers"—Schau did not take Beethoven's melody at its face value, whatever that wily Minister sings deserves our suspicion.

Christoph von Dohnanyi did not believe in Fernando's humanity either, when he not only conducted but also staged *Fidelio* in Frankfurt (1976). He, too, considered the Minister a hypocrite. In any event, the conclusion is ambivalent: political oppression evidently will continue.

In the Weimar production directed by Harry Kupfer (1969), Don Fernando's honor was restored. His arrival was interpreted, in line with Beethoven's intent, as a signal for the advent of a world of fraternity and humanity, as well as an appeal for "revolutionary action." The Minister, apostle of this idea, was pushed on stage in a cart which displayed a *tableau vivant* after Delacroix's famous panting of the French Revolution, complete with sansculottes, canons, and tricolor. Ernst Bloch once spoke in this connection of the " 'Marseillaise' above the fallen Bastille."

Kupfer gave Jaquino a new profile not justified on musical grounds: he no longer was the youthful lover but an elderly, bespectacled pedant who, when there was a knocking at the door, no longer received pointless packages but rather newly delivered prisoners. The Pizarro machine functioned. We used to call that mass arrest. Up to the beginning of the second finale, the scenic background was a brick prison wall. Marzelline dried her laundry on a line strung between posts holding chains for the prisoners. For the quartet, a table, chairs, and a few potted roses were brought in, props that were removed again at Pizarro's entrance. The final scene was dominated by a sun that broke through the clouds. Pizarro made a last stand, but was finally convinced by the threatening populace that his power was at an end. In the course of events, Rocco was also reexamined until he stood revealed before us as a henchman of violence, symbolizing a despicable fellow traveler of an authoritarian regime.

Friedrich Dieckmann labored over a new version of the *Fidelio* dialogues. He incorporated into the prose text a fuller account of the antecedents of the operatic action, its social background, and, above all, an exposé of Pizarro's shabby past. This criminal had once been a tax collector in Andalusia and as such had amassed a tremendous fortune through corruption. The farmers were hungry; they even revolted. Florestan stood by the disinherited; he wanted to unmask Pizarro. The latter anticipated Florestan's action and threw him into the deepest dungeon. Meanwhile, the Spanish king (was it Charles III?) reorganized his cabinet under pressure of the liberals. The result was political amnesty. To save his hide, Pizarro wanted quickly to dispose of the principal witness, Florestan. But in the nick of time, the newly named minister, Don Fernando, appeared as a deus ex machina, and the fury of the people swept away the antisocial Pizarro. Through his emendations, Dieckmann effectively eliminated those absurdities which censorship had imposed on the Treitschke libretto. Moreover, he skillfully removed the stilted pathos of the original libretto.[6]

However it is a fact that an opera audience cares little for intellectual motivations. The subscribers, who primarily attend the opera to hear the music, are not interested in Pizarro's bank account. They also have no great curiosity as to how he acquired his fortune. Decisive are the characters: a man who suffers; a woman who wants to end this suffering; and a criminal whose schemes ultimately collapse. Here we can learn from baroque dramaturgy. Even Euripides was partial to the deus ex machina, and Greek "opera" accepted it without question. Circumstantial motivations are tedious in a musical work of art. We are eagerly waiting to hear whether the soprano and tenor are able to cope with their high notes. Not that our intelligence is shut off, but it functions as—artistic intelligence. I do not know whether Dieckmann's version was adopted by German opera houses.

Let us return for one last time to skepticism. When Nikolaus Lehnhoff produced the opera in Bremen (1979), he removed the dialogue sections and replaced them with connecting texts written by Hans Magnus Enzensberger. The new texts were spoken by a basso who sat in the front row of the orchestra and who, at the finale, turned out to be the Minister and as such finally climbed up on the stage. Enzensberger admitted, as could be expected, that he mistrusted opera as an art form, and that he was not in sympathy with Beethoven's message of salvation. In one of his connecting texts he says: "Opera is an impossibility consisting of music, lights, and canvas." And later: "Opera is the realm of make-believe." We are therefore right in holding it suspect. Ergo, the *Fidelio* message is a deception. Prisons are still in our midst. *Fidelio* is nothing more than a Utopia. Enzensberger thinks that even Beethoven must have known that, for he wrote the music in a period of political reaction.

Günther Uecker created the scenery for Bremen, a study in chiaroscuro. At the beginning, a ray of light oscillated above the prison—a metronome of death or a ray of hope? Pizarro's henchmen carried lances inlaid with mirrors, which made the lances glitter even in the dark. Finally, a "path of light" pointed the way to freedom for the reunited couple. The color for the finale was white. The chorus, costumed in white, walked toward the audience with a gesture expressing *"Seid umschlungen, Millionen!"* Even Pizarro was allowed to sing along. For my taste, brotherhood was carried a bit too far.

Günther Rennert produced *Fidelio* three times in Salzburg. In 1948 a postwar mood prevailed. "The realistic atmosphere of the concentration camps and the deliverance by a liberal authority became the central concept of the production."[7] In 1948, such reference to the recent German past was inevitable.

Twenty years later, the enormous stage of the New Festival Playhouse shaped the production by Rennert and his designer, Rudolf Heinrich. A small part of the monstrous stage was set aside as Rocco's private sphere: it was not an interior but the front yard of a farm. An enormous sky arched over it. There was no awareness of a prison. When the set was revealed it floated, so to speak, in the air and was no preparation for what was to come. (In Berlin, 1937, Emil Preetorius solved the problem better by keeping the prison ever present.) In Salzburg, the entire width of the stage was then mobilized for a gigantic prison courtyard. What a hypertrophy of the scenic element! A film producer like Fritz Lang would have felt at home here. Nature was nowhere to be seen. The prisoners could warm themselves only on the music. For the second finale, the chorus received a visual extension through a relief of white figures, a "Millions, myriads, rise and gather!" made of canvas, plaster, and cardboard, thirty-five meters across the width of the stage. The idealistic German concept of liberty, from which Beethoven's music drew its strength, was demonstrated beyond a doubt. The C-major overture started at the end of the prison scene, the curtain remaining open while the couple slowly climbed the stairs to freedom.

Two years later, *Fidelio* arrived at the Felsenreitschule. Again Rennert had to face the challenge of an outsized stage. This time he solved the problem by dispensing with scenery altogether. The action, devoid of time and place, unfolded on and in front of a central podium. A solitary tree became meaningful to the chorus of prisoners. Great emphasis was placed on lighting design. For the finale, extras were used in the arcades of the Mönchsberg. (Back in 1957 von Karajan, in his *Fidelio* production, had used the arcades in the same manner.) On the whole, it was a static production which approached oratorio. This time Rennert wanted no allusions to politics; he even dissociated himself from idealistic pathos. He was now solely concerned with the personal suffering of the protagonist. Perhaps he wanted to return to Bouilly's *L'amour conjugal* or, even farther back, to the true story which had inspired the French librettist to write his *Léonore*. For that, a smaller stage would have served the producer better.

Mahler's Vienna *Fidelio* marked the start of our survey. It seems fitting to return to the birthplace of this opera. Two Viennese productions were memorable.

Napoleon's troops occupied Vienna when *Leonore I* had its unfortunate premiere. The Viennese of 1955 looked back on ten years of occupation by the Four Powers. Now they had departed, and the Staatsoper destroyed in a bombing attack in 1945, celebrated its reopening. The first evening in the restored house was devoted to *Fidelio*. Karl Böhm conducted; Heinz Tietjen directed; the decor originated with the architect Clemens Holzmeister, who could be expected to put a solid bastion on the stage. His prison scene was an almost baroque extravagance. Piranesi redivivus.

On this particular 5 November, the auditorium was filled with an affluent society, not necessarily Austrian. The Viennese, Phaeacians that they are, voiced their pride and enthusiasm in front of loudspeakers posted in the streets of their liberated city.

What happened in Vienna in 1970 when an authentic *Fidelio* was given during the annual Spring Festival? Leonard Bernstein conducted with such emotional involvement that there was concern for his health. Otto Schenk, who has no fear of realism and no standing with the avant-garde, was entrusted with the direction. Günther Schneider-Siemssen, who has no aversion toward romanticism either, was called in as designer. Here was a team that renewed the "Principle of Hope." Here one could anticipate an evening during which not only Beethoven but opera as an art form would come into its own. The world seemed whole once more when the big drawbridge was lowered. The success was questioned by only a few disgruntled critics who babbled about a "first-class funeral," and clamored for a "relevant" *Fidelio*. They must have been homesick for Kassel and Wuppertal.

The end of the Leonore story is not yet in sight. The search for relevance continues. When Wagner's great-grandson Gottfried made his directorial debut with *Fidelio* (Bonn, 1977), the listeners in the city of Beethoven's birth were not spared this quest for relevance. Gottfried found fault with the dialogues. Those he preserved, he updated. He put the third *Leonore* overture at the end of the opera, and whoever happened to be on stage at the time had to sit down on the floor, as if for a picnic; even Pizarro who, all evening long, had behaved like a Mafia boss, now had to listen to the music. Despite the C-major jubilation, the director insisted on his message in a minor key: evil can propagate, even if the opera closes with heavenly harmonies; political inhumanity makes progress in the world in which we opera lovers live. In any case, Gottfried here assured himself of Brecht's posthumous approval.

Der Freischütz

Max, a ranger in Duke Ottokar's service, was a profoundly honest but unstable, romantic character. An envoy from hell (Kaspar) persuaded him to employ diabolic arts in order to make sure that he would, by a master shot, win for his bride Agathe, the head ranger's daughter. Theatrical high point of the opera: the eerie scene in the Wolf's Glen where the magic bullets were cast. J. F. Kind's libretto is better than its reputation. He found the plot in a collection of ghost stories. Weber made important changes in the text. Kind had a prologue, in which a pious hermit, aiming to divert the catastrophe, handed a bouquet of blessed roses to the bride. Weber did not compose the prologue; the entrance of the hermit at the end of the opera is therefore unprepared. Kind once explained the idea of the libretto as follows: "The main thought, on which the entire fable is based, is that the evil principle strives to injure and ensnare even the pious; but a higher, wise, and humane power counteracts the evil."[1] Leibnitz's "pre-established harmony" still found believers in 1821. We are still in the magic circle of *The Magic Flute*. The good principle triumphs, the evil one lands in hell, and in both cases there are talismans (flute, roses). But the coloration of the orchestra has changed. The dark tones for the Wolf's Glen were not yet on Mozart's palette. Only Weber knew how to mix the colors for the pleasant aroma as well as the murky aspects of the German forest, which in this opera is, so to speak, the "leading character." At a time when Spontini defended his last stand on the Berlin operatic scene, Weber envisioned a new future of musical drama.

The production problems that emerged in our century betray a deep distrust of the romantic. Who still believes in the scares of the Wolf's Glen when terror reigns on the streets? Who nowadays is comfortable when he sees the subjects of a German princeling, huntsmen and peasants, sing jolly songs and dance the waltz? This discomfort shall be discussed on the following pages.

Where to start? With the "Hoftheater productions," so much maligned today? Beware of making fun of them: in no way did they spoil the pleasure that generations of opera lovers derived from Weber's music. After all, the premiere of *Der Freischütz* took place in a Hoftheater, in the august building designed by Schinkel in 1821 on the Gendarmenmarkt in Berlin. Here a tradition was established in Weber's view and hearing, retaining its validity for more than a century. Nobody was as yet ashamed of the Wolf's Glen owl with its "fiery, wheeling eyes"; the black boar still raced wildly across the stage; the waterfall still roared; the moon shone brightly into Agathe's room, turning dark during the ritual of the magic bullet; and the German forest was still full of secrets and dangers. These things are anchored in Weber's score: whoever is ashamed of them had better leave the work alone. But our directors have been ashamed of them and still produced *Der Freischütz*.

Let us begin with Rabenalt. He staged his disbelief in the romantic in Würzburg (1926) and three years later in Darmstadt. To be sure, in his promptbook notations he emphasized how close to nature Weber's music was, and said that "nature [had to] grow gigantically" from the production, as an "omnipotent force of fate."[2] But in practice he stifled Weber's feeling for nature, in

Würzburg as well as in Darmstadt. There was little evidence of nature in Rabenalt's decor. The trees seemed defoliated. A stylized staircase led up to Samiel's rock. In Darmstadt a screen was placed in front of this unimaginative background, which depicted the walls of the ranger's house most prosaically.

When German directors decide to put Weber's opera on their calendar they invariably do so with a bad conscience. They feel they have to apologize to the audience for the naive plot. Their discomfort manifests itself in psychological or socio-critical contortions. There is no lack of essayists to provide dramaturgic munition. Theodor W. Adorno was among them. In one of his *Moments musicaux* he discovered "an unresolved sexual symbolism" in Agathe, and a Max whose shot was the equivalent of a "defloration. . . . The allusions to sex are, at the same time, allusions to the decline of the bourgeois condition." The bridal chorus sounded somewhat "pallid and ominous" to him; it is even considered a "death symbol." In short: "All this has the aura of children's books from an earlier period."[3]

Adorno had hardly pronounced the words "children's books" when Harry Buckwitz picked up the idea for his Frankfurt production (1966) and decided to create his own kind of romantic, namely picture-book romantic. He told his designer, Schneider-Siemssen, to get some suggestions for the forest from Theodore Rousseau; everything visual was to be of a "disarming naiveté." The outcome was no German forest. The stylized trees created distance where closeness was desirable. Buckwitz expected that his picture book would emit a naive magic, "which would permit a smile rather than a jeer at what was meant seriously." To make his intention clear, the director opened each act with a *tableau vivant* that only came to life at the start of the music. Incidentally, a strange Hermit stepped out of this Frankfurt picture book. Buckwitz saw him as "a sly, rambunctious deus ex machina," a kind of Brother Cellarer, and in no way the representative of the preestablished harmony in which Weber undoubtedly had believed. From the program notes Buckwitz could have gathered that Weber considered his talent a gift from God, and that for the success of his opera God alone was to be praised. Weber took the message of salvation seriously, just as he took seriously the threat from satanic powers that ensnare man and from which he can only escape by the grace of God. The most important part in the libretto for Weber, as he explained in his conversations with J. C. Lobe, was the passage sung by Max: "I am enmeshed by treacherous powers."[4] To show the workings of these demons, Weber used the lowest register of the clarinet, the lamenting sound of the bassoon, and the dark roll of the kettle drum. The gemütlichkeit of the philistine *Biedermeier* atmosphere is built over chasms of which Weber was as aware as Grillparzer, Mörike, or Raimund.

Critics called the Frankfurt production "ingenious." To me this picture-book irony seems nothing more than a misplaced gag. No further development could be expected from it.

To look ahead, we first have to go back to Walter Felsenstein's production in the Komische Oper (Berlin, 1951). While the director was working on his concept, Karl Schönewolf, in the introduction to the Reclam libretto, opened his war against the "prettification, bagatellization, and petit-bourgeois philistinization" to which Weber's opera had been exposed for decades by "productions in courtly theaters."[5] In one respect Schönewolf was right: *Der Freischütz* was traditionally rendered innocuous. But what remedy did the East Berlin critic prescribe? First of all, he pointed out to the subscribers who pilgrimaged to Felsenstein that Kind had specified the time of the action as "'shortly after the Thirty Years War." Schönewolf exhorted the directors to take this time element to heart, and literally so, for this "postwar play" mirrors what the critic calls "the German calamity." In such a historical perspective Kaspar must be redefined. He was no longer the principle of unalloyed evil, in bondage to the "black ranger," Samiel, but "a barbaric mercenary, whom the war threw out of kilter." Max, although a ducal ranger, was "the son of a peasant people who are kept in ignorance by the reigning duke." That brings us right into the center of historical, social criticism. Schönewolf sees here an opportunity to demonstrate the contrast between the "impoverished, exploited peasants and the self-satisfied crowd of feudal rangers in their red coats." I make all the required efforts but do not succeed in discovering in the Bohemian waltz (no. 3) a trace of "exploited" peasants. The chorus of rangers (no. 15 in the score) does not impress me as being sung by "complacent mercenaries." Schönewolf focuses on the moral lesson of Kind's story, which is based on Apel's *Gespensterbuch*, by saying that "human happiness must not be made to depend on the trajectory of a bullet." This comes close to a Brechtian *Lehrstück*. The Hermit (to whom we owe the abolition of the test shot) in Felsenstein's version a youthful character, was no social reformer or pacifist, but the "blesséd of the Lord" the text calls for. The radiant ending in C major—Weber called it once the "transfiguration"—does not represent "social reason" but the affirmation of faith in Providence, a faith which asserted itself convincingly in Agathe's Cavatina (no. 12).

When Felsenstein produced *Der Freischütz* in Stuttgart (1967), his audience was a "consumer society."[6] The director had announced in his program notes that he would maintain a "critical distance" from the opera. Again sociological and ideological contortions seemed to be in the offing. But the result was different. This time nothing interfered with enjoyment. The director did justice to realism in portraying the world of the peasants and woodsmen, and he took the romantic of the Wolf's Glen seriously. He ignited the explosive material which Kind and Weber had placed between the characters. Nothing was left of routine movements save the round dance of the bridesmaids. These young girls were, after all, nontragic characters of Ännchen's kind. They, too, have a voice in the *Biedermeier* cosmos. In any case, Felsenstein had the score in mind, which cannot be said about too many directors today. The Stuttgarters, a people whose basic artistic orientation is culinary, had feasted at Weber's table. Felsenstein had seen to it during week-long rehearsals.

We are only at the beginning of the *via dolorosa* of this opera. Yet unforeseen aspects of socio-criticism were to be discovered in this early romantic wonderwork. In 1971 an important occasion presented itself: *Der Freischütz* celebrated its 150th birthday. East of the Berlin Wall hearty efforts were set in motion to "rejuvenate" this opera. It all started with a production by Ruth Berghaus (East Berlin, 1970). Brecht, her preceptor, had proclaimed: "Tradition is humdrum." Therefore Weber's romantic opera had to be newly conceived. What emerged from Unter den Linden was the demonstrated disbelief in a work which hitherto only philistines had taken seriously. In an effort to take remedial measures, the Berghaus conception aimed at the ironization of Kind's libretto. This came close to parody, and it was a pity that Nestroy had missed an opportunity here. The German forest was thoroughly cut down. At least, it was no longer green, and the head ranger's old house was obviously dilapidated. Even Wolfgang Lange, who usually has great patience with East German experiments, was taken aback.[7] It seems he didn't recognize Agathe. She had been devaluated: she wore an ugly *Biedermeier* hairdo, and on her belt hung a key ring and a mirror—she was a vain cow, with a "pinched, pale face, and a masklike grimace." Her Cavatina was made ridiculous by banal gestures. Alienation was in action. Max appeared "intellectually limited, unstable, and awkward." The Hermit was simply senile. Only the peasant dance à la Brueghel remains memorable.

What happened when producers began to look "behind the wings" of Kind's text? Unforeseen vistas opened up. To Max and Agathe no further harm could be done. Now the time had come to scrutinize that head ranger Kuno and his "Bohemian duke" Ottokar.

Kuno had inherited the office of head ranger. It was a family tradition. He has no son to take over the position, only a daughter, Agathe. Duke Ottokar was willing to pass the office on to Kuno's son-in-law, provided that Max proved himself in the shooting contest, the difficulty of which depended on the absolutist whim of the Duke. If one pays close attention to the dialogue, it becomes obvious that Kuno was more interested in the successor to his post than in the happiness of his daughter. We are dealing here with a rather contemptible individual, such as could develop ostensibly only during the Age of Absolutism.

The Duke is not spared, either. It is assumed that princelings of his kind had mistresses, and the Weimar production (1971) under Harry Kupfer's direction allotted him a pair of these ladies. He was dressed up in a costume fit to arouse the envy of Louis XIV. In Potsdam (1971), he also appeared as a fop. His huntsmen, arms at the ready, seemed to regret that the war had lasted a mere thirty years. In Dresden, Ottokar (with his mistresses) even appeared in a gilded coach. One could hardly expect him to follow the advice of the Hermit. Of course, this pious recluse had to be reevaluated also in East Germany. If he was senile in Berghaus's production, he became rejuvenated in Dresden, and in Potsdam he even turned into a nature boy. He was certainly no member of a religious order, rather an apostle of humanitarianism. In Weimar, to keep the modern audience's mind riveted on the horrors of war, Callot's "The Hanged" was projected onto the cyclorama, which gave the rustic jollity of the first act a rather ominous background, one calling for reflection. A cripple, obviously a war victim, dragged himself across the stage on his knees.

The *Freischütz* jubilee (1971) was not ignored by the Metropolitan Opera. Rudolf Heinrich was called in as director and designer in the hope that he would conjure an authentic *Freischütz* onto the stage. This expectation was dashed. The dialogues had been drastically shortened, so that the musical numbers followed in rapid succession without the necessary psychological preparation for their entry. The New York Wolf's Glen held no terror; rather, it elicited involuntary smiles.

Otto Schenk did a better job in Vienna (1972). He knew how, by employing all the modern stage techniques, he could do justice to the Wolf's Glen. Perhaps he overreached himself. He, too, might have sensed that our relationship to the romantic is uneasy. But he went full steam ahead, as is his wont. The Thirty Years War was relegated to the history books. A realistic style made the fable credible, and the appearance of the Hermit was given the importance which the music underlines. We surmised again what Weber must have meant, when he spoke of "transfiguration."

Further German experiments could be mentioned. For the pro-

73

duction in the baroque theater in Ludwigsburg Castle (1974) the director, Ernst Poettgen, had the idea (he is one of the directors who are full of ideas, i.e., gimmicks) to put the orchestra on the stage, behind the acting area. The chorus was removed to a balcony from which it not only sang but also commented on the action. The goal was alienation. It was reached without any difficulty.

In Ulm (1974) the opera was likewise mistreated. Giancarlo del Monaco eliminated the woods as "too romantic." Samiel was also fired. The Hermit had to abdicate in favor of a "Voice of Reason." The Wolf's Glen became Agathe's nightmare, and the bridesmaids crept around the bride in ominously synchronous rhythm, as though they were the Erinyes.

In Freiburg (1976) Michael Rothacker transposed the action into the nineteenth century. Agathe's pious faith was contagious. The head ranger's household was extremely religious. There was not only a house altar but also a prominent cross. No wonder, then, that in the Wolf's Glen a black mass was celebrated. The wild chase was eliminated; instead there was a monk who flagellated a naked girl. The Hermit seems to have died in the meantime. Since somebody had to lead the action to a happy conclusion, a priest appeared, passing by accidentally after officiating at a funeral.

In 1976 Götz Friedrich attempted *Der Freischütz* in Hamburg. In this production the war had just ended, which could only mean that the woods have been destroyed and that Schneider-Siemssen had to produce a barren landscape and a war-damaged ranger's house. The question is what has all this to do with a score ignorant of the horrors of war, but wise in the depth and confusions of human existence; a score that spoke of the good and evil powers that struggled for Max's soul? Friedrich had once more overeaten from the tree of knowledge.

Weber once said of his opera: "It contains terrible tasks."[8] Since he composed his opera before Karl Marx began to think, he could have shown little understanding of the methods by which our star directors strive to fulfill these tasks. Two so-called Hoftheater productions came, perhaps, closer to the solution. We already talked about Schenk's in Vienna. Now Gustav Sellner's West Berlin production (Deutsche Oper, 1966) deserves our attention.

Sellner came very close to Weber's spirit, although it could hardly have been expected from this very cerebral director. He had his designer, Jörg Zimmermann, conceive a decor that was dominated by the woods; even inside the ranger's house the forest atmosphere was noted. To underline the battle between good and evil, Sellner staged, after the overture, the spoken prologue, "The Roses of the Hermit," which Weber had not composed. That preserved the dignity and function of the recluse. Consequently, his presence was felt throughout the opera. At his second entrance he no longer has the effect of a deus ex machina: with his gift of the consecrated white roses he had diverted the calamity in the very prologue. Did not Weber exhort us in his final chorus "to trust firmly in the guidance of the Eternal?"

The Flying Dutchman

While the *Freischütz* legend was rooted in the forest, the *Holländer* myth emerged from the sea. Wagner had given precise instructions for the staging of the nautical scenes: "The director is to pay special attention to the ships and the sea. He will find all necessary instructions at pertinent places in the piano arrangement or the score." In the nineteenth century directing as we understand—or misunderstand—it today did not exist. Wagner had to rely on the ingenuity of his stage designer and of the mechanic. He also depended on the "lighting technician," who had to attend to the "nuances of the weather in the first act." Wagner had suggested to him that, through "clever use of painted scrims all the way up to the middle of the stage," the atmosphere required by the score should be given stage presence.[1]

A stage manager, a decorator, a mechanic, and a lighting technician—this quartet was responsible for a production. In our century the situation has changed. Now the director, if not an autocratic conductor, has the first and last word. *The Flying Dutchman* of the Krolloper (Berlin, 1929) may serve as an example. Klemperer conducted after he had already determined the character of the production by the choice of his scenic collaborators: he hired Jürgen Fehling from the legitimate stage as director; and as designer Ewald Dülberg, who came from the Bauhaus, where the students were not screened for their musicality. That trio obviously could not sympathize with Wagner's insistence on illusion. Dülberg facilitated the landing of the two seafarers, the Dutchman and Daland, considerably: there were no longer any dangerous cliffs, but cubistic shapes and comfortable stairs, inspired by Appia's "rhythmic spaces." One Berlin critic was reminded of a Hamburg pier. Another assured his readers: "Nobody gets seasick here, except the Wagnerian." The storm raged, though only in the orchestra pit; the ships were out of danger. Wagner's admonitions—"The sea between the islets must be portrayed as wild as possible," and "The treatment of the ship can not be too naturalistic"—fell on deaf ears. He had made every effort to inspire the director with textual as well as musical hints. Just one example of the composer's concern with "the strict interrelation of action and music": between the two stanzas of the helmsman's song is a *crescendo molto* of the cellos and the bassoons; Wagner wanted to see here its scenic equivalent—"Little details, like the shudder of the ship from the impact of a strong wave, must be drastically staged." Wagner's theatrical optics offer a brilliant analysis of the first entrance of the Dutchman. Every note in the score acquires a scenic meaning. There is no room for improvisation; everything is calculated.

All that was ignored at the Krolloper. The audience did not become acquainted with the dread of the sea; rather, perhaps, with the dread of lostness. "Black color inspires fear." This was, after all, the height of the expressionist period. Fehling directed as though he were dealing with Barlach. The Dutchman and Senta found themselves "in the paroxysm of their desire." Hysterical ecstasy was demanded of Senta. Strindberg was in the air she breathed, while spinning threads and thoughts in a kind of log cabin overshadowed by the contours of ghostly ships. The girls wore simple smocks and pullovers. Not all sat at spinning wheels;

some repaired nets, for which Wagner had not provided a musical equivalent. A pale light fell on the group which did not enjoy any gaiety.

Two years earlier, in Würzburg, Rabenalt had eliminated the "Norwegian idyll." He saw in these spinning girls "emaciated, proletarian victims of difficult living conditions." Hence the spinning song was sung without joy, although the wheels were gaily purring in the orchestra. Senta's ballad was supposed to "grow out of this unhealthy, sickly atmosphere."[2]

Rabenalt's concept indubitably rubbed off on the Klemperer production. It should also be mentioned, because it disconcerted the spectators, that the Kroll Dutchman did not wear a beard. His face, covered with white makeup, gave him a ghostly appearance. With that a tradition was broken, and from then on even Wotan had to shave. There were also musical surprises, for Klemperer conducted the original "brassy" Dresden version which Wagner had disavowed ten years later in Zurich. The composer had then changed the instrumentation of the overture by replacing the harsh brass, mostly trombones, with woodwinds and string instruments, and added the sound of the harp for the final redemption. There was no redemption for Klemperer. It was impossible to tell what was signified by the menacing fireball which rose from the traproom as the opera came to a close.

The composer had left to his grandson Wieland some archetypical suggestions for the interpretation of the Dutchman legend. According to those, the character of the Dutchman was determined "by the desire for peace after the storms of life." Richard Wagner saw in this desire an "age-old characteristic of human existence" (are we getting close to Jung?), such as found Grecian expression in Odysseus and Christian form in the Wandering Jew. Of course, Odysseus was no help for Wieland, who might have thought of Ahasuerus in passing. The suffering Prometheus also came to his mind: his Dutchman seemed nailed to the mast, crucified like Christ. The grandson reached back to his grandfather's "longing for peace," and in his Bayreuth production (1959) he found in the sea "the element of unrest," in the love of woman "the element of rest." His Dutchman was characterized by restlessness paired with an almost obsessive desire for permanence. For his conception of Senta, Wieland again went to the composer for advice. Richard Wagner's Senta was a "robust, Nordic girl," naive, not sentimental. The grandson guided the singer in this direction. "Nor must Erik be a sentimental whiner," declared the composer, who wanted to see this role played "stormily, violently, and darkly." Wieland molded his Erik in this fashion; a man driven by constant restlessness, hunter and hunted at the same time. Daland was likewise revalued and brought closer to the concept of Richard Wagner, who had warned against giving the captain too much comic leeway. "He is a coarse representative of common life." Wieland did away with the traditional good-natured philistine: his Daland became a contemptible "merchant of souls." In this connection and in view of all later attempts at devaluation, it is remarkable that Wagner, who, while he composed this opera, had taken pleasure in studying Proudhon, did not object to "the sale of a daughter to a rich man." Wagner's comment: "He thinks and acts like innumerable men, without suspecting evil." The nineteenth century still protected such a character, the twentieth called him to account: now ownership became theft.

Wieland Wagner gave the sea its due. He had not forgotten that once his grandfather had personally experienced its frights, during a trip from Riga to London. The choruses in Bayreuth were directed choreographically; their crowd in rhythmic motion suggested the pitching of the ship. A magnificent drill performance. Unforgettable also was the invasion of the lemurlike Dutch crew against the background of a phosphorescent skeleton, a sort of X-ray of the phantom ship.

Some critics applauded Wieland's return to "realism." It was a magic realism. The beardless Dutchman elicited no comment. The uniformly dressed and emphatically top-heavy spinning girls were an embarrassment. The picture of the Dutchman did not hang in the room but rather above the rafters, so that only Senta, who was clairvoyant, could see it; the picture faded out when the real

Dutchman entered the stage. All this was laudable. Our reservations are directed against the finale.

There was no question of redemption. The Dutchman died, evidently damned, before he reached his ship. Senta ran along a side gallery, helplessly groping her way, and gave her promise of faithfulness before she collapsed. There was no "glowing red" of the rising sun, no "blinding glory," such as the scenic fantasy of the composer had suggested. What was on Wieland's mind when he conceived his method of ending the opera? He once commented on it in a later interview: "I did not ignore [the theme of redemption], I simply interpreted it differently, namely as referring solely to the love of woman. It can, without difficulty, be understood that way."[3] The audience, uninitiated in the director's thought processes, of course could not "understand it that way," and was inclined to consider the final arrangement as a capitulation before technical exigencies. Thus a part of the Dutchman's curse remained unexpiated.

The curse remained active and finally reached the Vienna Staatsoper, where Gertrud Wagner, Wieland's widow, produced the opera in 1967, "after Wieland Wagner," as the program notes said. Now much seemed petrified, and much gave rise to unintended drollery. One innovation: the picture of the Dutchman was projected on a scrim stretched in front of the stage. During the rehearsals there had been a quarrel between Frau Wagner and Anja Silja (Senta), who thereupon resigned. The opera rowdies, who are part of the regulars attending the Vienna Opera, protested by hooting and whistling. In the middle of such a circus atmosphere it was difficult to be interested in the Dutchman's fate.

So far *The Flying Dutchman* is the only Wagner opera produced by the Komische Oper in East Berlin. Joachim Herz, in his 1962 production, left legendary Norway. He demythologized it thoroughly. For Herz, the opera was not timeless; he set it at the time of its composition—i.e., during the 1840s, in a milieu such as might have been Ibsen's when he grew up. The Dutchman enters the philistine Daland world as a "stranger." Daland, in his *Bie-*

dermeier costume with tails and top hat, becomes the archetype of the "greedy, bourgeois entrepreneur." He does not sail on an obsolete caravel, but travels on a sailing ship with steam engine. In this prosperous captain's home—amply furnished by Rudolf Heinrich—young ladies of the middle class meet for a sort of coffee klatch. All this Herz views with skeptical social criticism, and he points out that, during the time when Wagner composed the *Dutchman*, he had been reading anticapitalist writings. Senta wanted to break out of her stuffy environment. There was a germ of Hedda Gabler in her. She liked Erik the hunter because he, at least, was close to nature, though basically his horizon was limited.

This interpretation works for a while, yet in the end the redemption scene has to be managed. Herz could no more cope with it than could Wieland Wagner. In the Komische Oper, Senta suffered a stroke while the Dutchman was struck by lightning. To be sure, none of this is in the score.

It was expected that with Rudolf Sellner's production in the Deutsche Oper (1965) a new Wagner era would begin in West Berlin. It was a question of finding a line between tradition and neo-Bayreuth. Sellner succeeded by emphasizing the balladlike character of the action. This time the sea was included in the play. The visual star of the production was Teo Otto's spectral ship, first in its realistic presentation as a moldy wreck, later in its surrealistic form as a skeletal ship's hull. Sellner came pretty close to a production that did justice to the score.

This cannot be said of the London production (Covent Garden, 1966). Clifford Williams was responsible for the direction, which was under the spell of neo-Bayreuth. The stage designer, Sean Kenny, decided on a sloping platform, supposed to fulfill the scenic need of all three acts by tilting, lowering, or turning. It was asking too much. The sea was rough in the orchestra pit, while on the stage everything remained static. The demonic conductor, Georg Solti, must have felt this to be a break in the style. The ghost ship in no way resembled a seaworthy vessel. It did have a mast that looked like a gigantic phallus and ejaculated red rays.

After all, the Dutchman had not been ashore in seven years! No wonder it was mating season for the girls in Daland's home.

August Everding, who had earned his spurs as director on the legitimate stage, was called to Bayreuth in 1969 in order to produce a new *Dutchman* with the help of the Czech lighting magician, Josef Svoboda. The director frankly admitted that he had no ready-made concept in his pocket. Evidently he had not decided to delve into the mythical past but simply wanted to retell the fairy tale with a certain naiveté and without intermission.

Nobody had doubted that Svoboda would cope with the ghostly appearance of the phantom ship. Nor was there a lack of optical effects in the third part. If anything, he overdid them. The final picture was dominated by a steep outside staircase from which Senta performed her suicidal leap. Then the stage became brighter for the first time. That was the transfiguration. Svoboda's spinning room evidently served to dry nets which were used as borders. The Dutchman sang his great aria from the bow of the ghost ship. The composer had labored in vain when he musically underscored the sailor's first steps ashore.

Thanks to his unlimited power of imagination, Ulrich Melchinger thought up a totally new *Dutchman* for Kassel in 1976. How would it be, he speculated, if the Dutchman weren't "flying" at all, but a crafty marriage swindler who went from fishing village to fishing village, seduced the girls, and promised their fathers he would pay? As soon as discovery threatened, he terrified the good citizens by persuading them that he was in reality the "flying" Dutchman. Senta, who had never doubted that he was the "real" article, became the victim of Erik's knife when she threw herself between him and the swindler in order to protect the liar.

We naive mortals had always taken the entrance monologue of the Dutchman seriously. We pitied this Ahasuerus of the seas; we were under the spell of the music; we wanted to see the man redeemed who revealed his torment in his great aria. Lest the Kasselers attach bourgeois values to this aria, Melchinger strangely alienated it. As a diversion the Dutchman celebrated a black mass on deck, a blasphemy complete with skulls, call girls, and a naked woman, whom the swindler (evidently impotent), deflowers with his—sword.

Until now Wagner's opera had been considered a youthful work. It remained for Melchinger to degrade it to a juvenile opus. Such irony would have turned even Heine's stomach.

There are stage directors who seem to be more interested in Daland than in the cursed Dutchman. Dieter Bülter-Marell, who, as guest director in Wuppertal (1978), had the opportunity to prove himself with the *Dutchman*, was one of them. It had long been the fashion to produce operas in costumes of the time in which they were composed. That makes the Ahasuerus of the Sea no longer a timeless myth but a reality of the early capitalist period of 1840. The ostentatious Daland (as already with Herz in East Berlin) was not satisfied with a sailing vessel; he had a steamship, with auxiliary sails. The spinning wheels humming in his home were no longer driven by hand but by machine. Everybody acquainted with the score knows right away that there is no musical equivalent for such a mechanization. Anyway, in a romantic opera, who cares about Wagner's socio-critical attitude of the 1840s?

In 1978 it was time for Bayreuth again. Nine years had passed since Everding's *Dutchman*. It was replaced by Harry Kupfer's new interpretation. There had already been a black Venus on the festival hill; now for the first time, a black Dutchman stood on the Bayreuth stage, where the psychopathic concept of the director raged. It all began with the overture: we were not allowed to enjoy it as a pure piece of music, for there was not only something to hear but something to see as well: Senta sat in her attic chamber, her hair blown by the storm of the orchestra and the wind machine, dreaming about her Dutchman and, clairvoyantly, witnessing her father's first meeting with the Seeker of Redemption. Senta was in bad shape. Obviously, she had second sight. She pressed the portable picture of the Dutchman convulsively against her bosom. We had a hysterical Senta, one who could not cope with her neuroses. She should have seen a psychiatrist, but there were none in 1843. She did not even see the real Dutchman with whom, after all, she was singing a duet; she carried in her disturbed soul and at her breast the image of the wan seafarer. She sang of his deliverance, but the redemption through love did not take place. Senta committed suicide. She threw herself out of her attic window and lay dead on the pavement. Tableau. The Dutchman will have to wait another seven years until once more an angry sea throws him ashore. This time he was merely a supporting actor, existing only in Senta's schizophrenic daydreams.

Kupfer had decided to bring a "hard" *Dutchman* to the Bayreuth stage. He therefore chose (as had Klemperer) the original version which had no redemption. (The Bayreuth of today is not exactly redemptive.) So, the harpist had a day off. The brass section, on the other hand, worked overtime. Kupfer (or his conductor) had Senta sing her ballad in A minor. (Wagner had introduced the customary G-minor version for the sake of Mme. Schröder-Devrient.) This carried the redemption scene into a radiant C major, which was absurd inasmuch as Kupfer's interpretation did not allow for any C-major glory.

It should not be overlooked that the evening offered a whole series of surprises. For instance, the arrival of the ghostly ship: its bow opened to spew out a Dutchman who, in contradiction to the score, drunkenly tottered ashore. There were lightning-quick, surreal changes of cliffs and walls; and the strange alienation of the Norwegian sailors who, with chalk-white faces, appeared no less spooky than the crew of the phantom ship, although they had to sing in C major.

In conclusion: this *Dutchman* certainly did not sail around the Cape of Good Hope. It is one more fall from grace for the human intellect, a new symptom of hubris based on a total lack of musical understanding. How far removed all this was from the concept of Wagner, who had let his friend Ferdinand Heine know that he hoped to transmit to his listeners "the entire aroma of the myth," and "to be able to hold them in that rare mood in which—with a minimum of poesy—one can grow to love the gloomy legend to the point where one finds it comfortable."[4] But who nowadays is endowed with "that minimum of poesy," and who is looking for comfort? Perhaps the minority of protesting spectators.

No more harm could be done to Senta: Kupfer had finished her off. The next director's basilisk glance fell on the harmless helmsman. Jean-Pierre Ponnelle had the idea first realized in San Francisco and then in the Metropolitan Opera (1979), to turn the action of the opera into a dream of the helmsman. Since dreams know no boundaries, the director made an excursion into no-man's-land. The scenery was never changed: for three acts we were confined to the deck of Daland's ship, where even the spinning wheels of the Norwegian girls were set in motion. Absurd, isn't it? Yes, but then, it was only a dream of the helmsman, who suddenly saw himself transposed into the role of Erik. Even Freud would have had a hard time coming up with an interpretation. The director of some third-rate provincial troupe who, trying to save on the fee for a second tenor and stinting on the decor, could not have done worse. The dream of the helmsman turned into a traumatic nightmare for the spectator.

Aida

It all began with a novella the Egyptologist Edouard Mariette had invented on the basis of Egyptian motifs. The fable fell into the hands of the viceroy of Egypt, Ismael Pasha, who had just built himself an opera house in Cairo and was on the lookout for a new opera. He entrusted Camille du Locle, director of the Paris Opéra Comique, with the task of fashioning a libretto out of the Egyptian story and finding a composer for it. Verdi was in Paris at the time and got interested in du Locle's scenario, although he insisted on finding his own librettist. Verdi's choice was Antonio Ghislanzoni, who had already delivered verses for the revision of *La sforza del destino*. The composer finished the demand opera in four months. But the Cairo premiere had to be postponed because in the meantime the Franco-Prussian war had broken out, leading to the siege of Paris. The scenery and costumes which the khedive had ordered and Mariette had supervised were locked in together with the Parisian populace. Mariette had seen to it that the scenery left nothing to be desired in respect to "Egyptian authenticity." It can no longer be ascertained which dynasty he had in mind; he had at his disposal a historic past of three thousand years. The premiere of the opera finally took place in 1871, two years after the opening of the Suez Canal.

For decades the spirit of Mariette hovered over the opera in every part of the world. Following the Cairo model, *Aida* remained an exotic showpiece. Not even Toscanini and Caruso could change that. An impresario, whose budget permitted horses, elephants, and camels on the stage for the triumphal march and who could point proudly to his "authentic" decors and costumes, was considered the chosen man to include this opera in his repertory.

Let us first consider the Metropolitan Opera, where Giulio Gatti-Casazza became director in 1908. He opened his first season with *Aida*. The critic of the *New York Times*, Richard Aldrich, was carried away by the spectacular settings: "The new management strained every nerve and put forward all its resources, apparently, to outdo all that had ever been done before in the way of painting the stage picture."[1] On this evening Toscanini made his debut at the Met. A musical revelation! Yet, it was the Egyptian museum on the stage that remained the talk of the town.

During the depression in the thirties the Met had a competitor in the Hippodrome, where Alfredo Salmaggi was the *Aida* expert. He saw in this opera possibilities for circus acts. In any case, he had more success in training the animals that he mobilized for his triumph, than in taming the singers. Those were the golden days of Sixth Avenue! Cecil B. De Mille must have been delighted.

Aida, understood as "Grand Opera," was eminently suited for Italian alfresco performances. In the Arena di Verona the opera was newly produced at least fifteen times with a maximum display of splendor. At a recent production (1969) Luciano Damiani cleverly exploited the enormous size of the stage for the two mass scenes: he had the Egyptian army march off on the uppermost tier of the arena at the end of the first ensemble scene, and had it reenter from there for the victory celebration. For the rest, Damiani had decided on an art-nouveau decor.

In the Roman Termi di Caracalla there were no such stylistic finesses and esthetic musings. But there was compensation though with a Radamès who, for the triumph, galloped on stage in a battle chariot drawn by four horses, a veritable quadriga. The spectators held their breath. At the beginning of the third act, while the music caught the mood of the moon-bathed Nile landscape (all instruments *con sordino* and above them the lonely voice of the flute), a supernumerary dressed as a fellah drove a camel across the stage. Whispers in the audience: *"Un camello!"*

Only after World War II did the Egyptian museum disappear from the operatic stage, when voices were heard that faulted the established conventions and wanted to liberate *Aida* from the curse of Grand Opera.

Wieland Wagner made the beginning in 1961, when he produced *Aida* at the Deutsche Oper in West Berlin as an "African mystery." He pointed at the overture which anticipates the two basic themes of the opera: the love motif of the violins (Aida's leitmotif), and the pithy theme of the priests with its mercilessly hard rhythm—love confronting a rigid system of order by which the lovers perished. They could only be united in death. Theirs, too, was a love death. Wieland called *Aida* Verdi's *Tristan*, the love relationship between Radamès and Aida "a passion of the soul," in contrast to Amneris's love, which was motivated by "unadulterated sensuality." For that reason Wieland put a huge phallus in Amneris's bedroom, commenting: "This gigantic phallus is Amneris's constant dream." She wanted to save Radamès from sentencing, through her influence as the King's daughter, "because only in his person can the dream of the gigantic phallus become reality."[2] This analytical playing on the priapic libido was actually quite unappetizing.

Wieland Wagner transformed the triumphal march, which traditionally parades in broad daylight, into a nocturnal nightmare. In Berlin, darkness reigned. To be sure, Wieland's theatrical nights are always filled with symbolism. He defended the gloomy atmosphere as follows: "From the moment when honor and duty to his country compel Radamès to renounce Aida, there can only be night in his soul. For him this night extends over the entire world." Not a trace of that can be found in Verdi's score. On the contrary. When, in the third act, Radamès confronted Aida alone for the first time, Verdi invented a heady, spirited love melody, to be sung *con trasporto*. There is no trace of Wieland's pessimist, Radamès.

The West Berlin triumphal scene was quite ethnographic. Ethiopian slaves lugged enormous totemic objects and African sculptures across the stage as part of the victors' booty. Suddenly we were in the deepest Congo. Nothing was left of Egyptian artwork. Wieland, as so often in his productions, aimed once more at the elementary, the original, the archetypical "basic situation" ("*Grundsituation*"), which this time was the foundering of love on the conflict between two cultures.

When Franco Zeffirelli produced *Aida* at the Scala in Milan (1963), he consciously countered Wieland's symbolism. He decided to evoke the historical style of the Cairo premiere (with the help of the sophisticated decors of Lila Di Nobili). Only spectators dressed in the fashion of Napoleon III were lacking. Zeffirelli was obsessed with the idea that the pharaohs' society he was dealing with was "saturated," a "dying world" with its "symptoms of decay." Had not just then, in 1870, the second empire collapsed? Whatever odor of decay it left behind, Verdi's music did not absorb any of it.

A Frankfurt revival was successful in 1966. Bohumil Herlischka, whose interest in opera always inspired a certain dread, for once did not shock his audience. He avoided all eccentricities and stayed within the frame of the prescribed plot, whose realistic aspects he wanted to bring to the fore. He instructed his stage designer, Teo Otto, to renounce historicizing display of pomp, and to create an ambiance in which the three main characters could develop psychologically. "The external splendor is to be exchanged for an X-ray picture that shows the abysmal dangers of that world in which Radamès and Aida move."[3] Those were Herlischka's demands, and Otto understood his task. This time it was Egypt that was dangerous, not the director.

When the Metropolitan Opera opened its new building in 1969 with *Aida*, it was once again "Grand Opera" in the traditional, static style of production. (Director, Nathaniel Merrill; stage designer, Robert O'Hearn.) From Rudolf Bing's point of view, the love story between an Egyptian general and an Ethiopian slave appeared entirely unproblematic. *Aida*—an opera that evidently caused trouble only for the designer. In 1974 a merciful fire consumed the costumes. The Met decided on a new production in 1976, which was to bring a decisive revision of the traditional mise-en-scène. The partners, James Levine and John Dexter, no longer envisioned "Grand Opera," they opted for "intimate opera." The crowd scenes were, after all, concentrated in the first act, and the triumph was in the second. For the most part it is the monologues, duets, and trios that promote the drama, and Levine and Dexter aimed at the drama, not at the spectacle. Both men considered the priests the real criminals. They were the warmongers and judges responsible for the catastrophe. The lovers were shown as victims of a totally ritualized society. Fascism was in the opera air, so Dexter directed the triumph as "a kind of fascist rally." Like Wieland Wagner, Dexter avoided radiant light. But where Wieland proffered psychological reasons, Dexter produced practical ones: in torchlight, fewer extras could create the illusion of a larger crowd. In his hatred of the priests, Dexter had overlooked the fact that it was the Ethiopians who had attacked the Egyptians. But who knows nowadays who started a war where? Besides, in operas (even in Verdi's) one should not be too inquisitive about such matters. The music, fortunately, keeps silent about them. Davis Reppa created the decors. The stage made a very bare impression. No pyramids or sphinxes in sight. In their stead monumental pictures of gods, appliquéd on a textile background, while the actual drama took place on a golden disk. The love tragedies of the captive Ethiopian as well as of the Egyptian royal daughter unfolded in a heartless environment.

In the Götz Friedrich production (Komische Oper, East Berlin, 1969), stage designer Reinhart Zimmermann expressed the coldheartedness of the priesthood through the use of aluminum sheeting.[4] There is nothing colder than metal, except perhaps the hearts of the ruling theocrats. Nothing remained of Egypt. The unlocalized opera had become "timeless." Even the proscenium was paneled with metal plates, some concave, some convex. This was continued on the stage, which was closed off in the back by an enormous metal piece. On the sides were smaller metal surfaces. The world of the clergy was congealed in the cold. When the metal background opened occasionally, we got a glimpse of the machinery and apparatus, "signals" for the activities of a pitiless technocratic regime. How to bring color into this tinny desert? Again Zimmermann knew what to do. He constructed a revolving, ocatagonal podium in which were set colored glass panes that could be illuminated from below. For the *"Celeste Aida"* the rotating octagon lit up when Radamès began his romance. Later Aida prayed on the same spot, and the Radamès color returned. During the torpid singing of Amneris (*"Vieni, amor mio"*) the podium glowed multicolored. In the Nile act there was no Nile, again nothing but metal and the shimmery, many-hued revolving podium.

Friedrich's production did not last long on the East Berlin stage. The director fell from grace, relocated in the West, and brought his *Aida* lock, stock, and barrel to the Holland Festival in Amsterdam. The Dutch bought the aluminum stage from the East Berliners, who were only too glad to get rid of it. The multicolored podium was also mounted in the Amsterdam Carré Theater, a former circus. Friedrich explained his directing concept to the festival audience: this opera was an enactment of "the collision between totalitarian, imperial power and the humane rebellion of the individual"—i.e., something we are used to finding in *Antigone*. During the triumph, the "system" is in full sway. For the older Dutch all this was recent past, these legions in black costumes, marching in lockstep, with their shouts of *"Guerra!"* or *"Gloria!"* on the one side, and on the other those wasted (Ethiopian?) slaves of the state who gained their freedom only in the opera. The three principals were broken characters from the start, every one enmeshed in insoluble conflict, near madness. The Dutch proved to be a grateful audience.

At times it seemd as if ancient Egypt could not be suppressed.

Sporadically it made a comeback on the stage. It appears that the law of gravity burdens *Aida*. The citizens of Hamburg have a tale to tell about that. In 1970, Filippo Sanjust once more offered an *Aida* straight out of the museum. There were again solid cardboard objects such as the bases of pyramids and the superdimensional feet of pharaoh statues. There also was a Nile of such breadth that it threatened to inundate the orchestra. The triumph achieved an especially realistic note: one of the priests distributed alms to the ragged crowd that gaped at the spectacle. This idea is on the same level as the Roman camel. The singers had a hard time competing with the scenic monumentality.

Monumental or intimate? Removed from time or close to it? The fate of this opera is in balance. I see no reason for neglecting the Egyptian components. After all, the libretto speaks of pharaohs, and at moments the music has a delicate, exotic flavor. Therefore the exotic element needs only to be hinted at by the designer. We have long outgrown the didactic museums-tour approach. However, a valid *Aida* model for our times is still lacking.

Carmen

There is a "soft" *Carmen* (lower- and upper-middle-class, romantic) and a "hard" *Carmen* (realistic, derived from Mérimée and
Nietzsche's admiration). Either variant can be justified on the basis
of the score. The listener who wants to enjoy his *Carmen* in a sentimental vein pays only fleeting attention to the fate motif and con-
centrates on the duet of Don José and Micaëla, the flower aria,
Micaëla's aria, and the prelude to the third act. The other party
points to Carmen's card monologue, the duel between Don José
and Escamillo, and the "hatred to death" of the sexes in the last
confrontation. This score is successful from the lyric as well as the
dramatic point of view. There are highlights in major and minor
keys, and Bizet, partially bound by tradition, partially looking into
the future, knew how to please every taste.

The stage career of this opera started inauspiciously in the Paris
Opéra Comique (1875). Both the audience and those responsible
for the production had trouble with the novel subject matter. One
Paris critic pinpointed the objections of the habitués when he
wrote: *"Quelle vérité, mais quel scandale!"* An opera with factory

girls, gypsies, whores, smugglers, and an AWOL soldier with a criminal record who finally becomes a murderer—this was not the fare one would expect at the Opéra Comique, this was "*le scandale*." At first, the work was not successful.

However, the very year of the Paris premiere, the production of the Vienna Hofoper helped *Carmen* to the worldwide fame which Paris had to confirm in its new production of 1883. In the original version of the opera, musical numbers alternate with spoken dialogue. For the Vienna production, Ernest Guiraud was asked to shorten the dialogues and change them into recitatives. They reached Vienna too late to be rehearsed, so that the first performance in the Hofoper still had the spoken dialogues (in watered-down German). Eventually, Guiraud's recitative version conquered the world simply because the singers could not reconcile themselves to the spoken word. Guiraud was also responsible for certain orchestral emendations which Bizet had not authorized, but which were nevertheless adopted in all the scores of Europe until Walter Felsenstein and his musical collaborators aimed at restoring the "Ur-form."

Carmen received its definitive scenic form in the Opèra Comique from director Albert Carré. Foreign visitors could not praise it enough. Carl Hagemann, general manager in Mannheim and Wiesbaden, was among the admirers.[1] Hans Gregor, who opened his Komische Oper in Berlin, 1905, was deeply impressed by the French style of directing and took up Carré's ideas (today one would call them "gimmicks") in his own *Carmen* production. What had Carré offered? He began by hiring two Spanish painters, Ignacio Zuloaga and Ermenegildo Anglada, who furnished the Mediterranean ambiance and the authentic costumes. The first decor showed with almost photographic fidelity a square in Seville. This was a feast for the eyes: supernumeraries buying oranges from a vendor; people strolling by; friends exchanging greetings; a lady appearing in her window looking for her lover, who eventually showed up bringing her roses. Other love affairs were initiated. A beggar was also essential for this Spanish milieu, and a few loafers who slept off the effects of their drinks. The soldiers played cards, smoked, read the newspaper. Later on fights began among the street urchins. This was Spain seen through French eyes.

Hans Gregor tried to compete with the French in his Komische Oper (Berlin, 1906). This called for a break with the routine that had been established on the German stage since 1875, a routine that had changed Carmen into a demimondaine in a pseudo-Spanish milieu. Gregor's production was a declaration of war against all traditions of the "soft" version. He had sent his stage designer, Karl Walser, for a few weeks to Spain so he could soak up the atmosphere. Walser's sketch for the first act showed a plain square into which narrow alleys led, with glaringly lighted yellow buildings against an intensive blue sky. There was also a barbershop. Gregor insisted on a bench or a fountain for the Don José-Micaëla duet—reminiscences of home are not to be exchanged standing up. Walser protested: any seating arrangement would disturb the simple lines of his design. The director gave in to the esthetic objections of his designer and thought of another solution. He brought in a cart with bags of flour; during the unloading, one of the bags fell down so that the couple could sit on it for their duet. The Berlin critic Fritz Jacobsohn, who, incidentally, was an admirer of Gregor, had the impression that here and elsewhere the staging offered too much of a good thing, which did not fit in with Bizet's "rather limited musical power."[2] Gregor, like Carré, took the soldiers' chorus too literally: "*Sur la place, chacun passe, chacun vient, chacun va.*" There were simply too many "*drôles de gens.*" Lillas Pastia's tavern was a real smugglers' haunt: "Old, dilapidated walls, the night sky visible through the roof, sparsely illuminated with three miserable oil lamps." The third act was also very effective: a steeply upward-sloping gorge whose rocks were placed far downstage. The smugglers groped their way in the dark from above and from the sides. Carmen sat in front of a glowing fire and read her fortune in the cards.

In Gregor's Komische Oper little importance was attached to bel canto. The accent was on character portrayal. Gregor never denied that he had served his apprenticeship as an actor with Otto Brahm, the naturalistic stage director, and he once remarked that he did not consider the road from Bizet to Gorki very long. It is typical of Gregor's style that, when searching for an assistant director, he thought of Richard Vallentin, a gifted actor in Max Reinhardt's ensemble. He was looking for an opera director who "if possible, had never seen an opera." He finally found a congenial collaborator in Maximilian Moris.

Carmen became visibly "harder" as the work fell into the hands of Vladimir Nemirovich-Danchenko, who in 1924 prepared a production entitled *Carmencita and the Soldier* in the Musical Studio of the Moscow Art Theater. He asked the Russian poet Constantin Lipskeroff to write a completely new text, firmly based on Mérimée and on Nietzsche's admiration for Bizet's music. Nietzsche was godfather to the central idea of this version when he wrote: "Love as fate, as fatality, cynical, innocent, cruel—and therefore natural. Love, whose means is war and whose foundation the mortal hatred of the sexes."[3] Reading Lipskeroff's libretto today, one is reminded of Lorca. Extreme demands were made on the supportive capacity of the music, especially since Vladimir Bakaleynoff proceeded like a vandal with Bizet's score when he reworked the music. The director went so far in his urge to "harden" the opera that he eradicated Micaëla: she was considered a concession to a bourgeois audience. Her function was arrogated by three female voices who took the place of José's mother, or, to express it differently, the principle of good which lay dormant in José's subconscious. There was also a women's chorus about which two Russian critics had the following to say, in the New York souvenir program: "This Chorus serves as a link between the audience and the heroic characters of the drama. Placed upon a high balcony overlooking the stormy scenes enacted below, the Chorus, aloof, impersonal, and prophetic becomes a spectator in the unfolding of events, commenting, warning, and foretelling, reinstated in its ancient tragic function." The stage designer Isaac Rabinovich built tiered constructs that only an unmusical brain could relate to Bizet's music. In 1925 the Russians brought their product to the West. The impression in Berlin? Alfred Kerr was enthusiastic, but we may dismiss his numbered exaltations. In New York, some were turned on, others turned off.

The next step toward a harder *Carmen* was again made in Berlin, this time in the Krolloper, where Ernst Legal worked out a new production in 1928. While the direction oscillated between melodrama and verism, the designs of Caspar Neher determined the basic tone of the production. His Seville was presented as a daringly constructed cliff city in dirty yellow. There was no blue sky. Something ominous emanated from the scenery, as if Neher had given visual expression to the fate motif. The mountain city rose also above Lillas Pastia's den. The last picture in chiaroscuro had only one color accent, a reddish-brown awning. Joy in colors was definitely not Neher's forte.

Before we pursue further the fate of the opera in Berlin, chronology takes us back to Moscow, where Stanislavsky, just prior to his death, produced a *Carmen* in his Opera Studio (1935).[4] Here we are with the father of "realistic musical theater" who occasionally forced his "system," developed for the legitimate stage, on the opera. The director wanted to scrape off the layers of varnish that had collected on this opera, even in Russia (Bolshoy Theater!). For him, *Carmen* was a "folk drama," a "popular soldier and peasant opera." He went back to Mérimée's novella and created from it a severe style of production that thoroughly did away with all the "bourgeois" operatic tinsel. The soldiers were in sleazy blue uniforms, the gypsies in rags, the children dirty; Don José was a village lad, Micaëla a peasant girl, who felt out of place in the urban environment. Carmen became "an enchanting vice," the "beautiful sin." Stanislavsky rightly emphasized the contrasting qualities on which he wanted the entire role to be based. As the setting for act 1, he demanded a popular street milieu. He intended to transplant the action of act 3 into a mountain city, with corridors hewn into the rocks for prowling smugglers and the duel between José and Escamillo. Snow was to cover the mountains.

Since Stanislavsky had read Mérimée, there was hardly a director who failed to prepare himself for his operatic task by studying the novella. Tyrone Guthrie should be mentioned here, who, after the war, produced the opera in Sadler's Wells. In Anna Pollak he found a singer who did not hesitate to portray Carmen as a "vulgar, violent slut." Correspondingly, Guthrie's Spain was no picture-postcard Spain: "The first act was set in quite a squalid, sordid sort of environment, and the factory girls looked like factory girls."[5] For the last act the director provided an innovation: instead of a public plaza in front of the bullring, Guthrie placed the last confrontation between Carmen and Don José in an interior with "no exit" for Carmen. Here Guthrie succumbed to the false assumption that Carmen would cry for help in a public square. He underestimated the significance of the fate motif: Carmen did not want to run away, she chose death.

From Stanislavsky it is a logical step to Walter Felsenstein's production (Komische Oper, East Berlin, 1949). He rejected the recitatives and reinstated the original version with the dialogues, which made the drift of the action clearer. Now details of Don José's past were uncovered: that he came from Navarre; that he had wanted to become a priest but did not like to study; that he had to flee his home on account of a fight; and more immaterial details. Felsenstein also offered a completely new German translation. Josef Fenneker's sets were determined by a stair motif. There was a staircase leading up to the cigarette factory; another one for Escamillo's entrance; stairs for the smugglers and stairs for the bullring. These stairs aided the director in realizing his ideas. He was indefatigable in the invention of realistic details. Every supernumerary had a role to play. Carré was outdone. Felsenstein achieved his goal: he tore the opera from the clutches of "bourgeois romantization," while Klemperer made it a point that no "soft" mood could originate in the orchestra pit.[6]

In 1969 Felsenstein produced the opera in Moscow, (Stanislavsky-Danchenko Theater) with Russian artists. These, too, were willing to subject themselves during weeks of rehearsal to the rules of realistic music theater which substantially differed from the Bolshoy Theater routine. In 1972 Felsenstein decided to refurbish his production at the Berlin Komische Oper. This time he imported from Moscow his Carmen, Micaëla, and Don José, who all had a tough time with the German dialogues. Wilfried Werz created new scenery which lacked a uniform style, but did get rid of Fenneker's staircases. The musical basis of the production was the score worked out, true to Bizet, by Fritz Oeser; the last traces of Guiraud were definitely expunged. Felsenstein breathed a sigh of relief. In a lecture given in 1972, he traced the "actual tragedy" of Carmen and Don José. In the course of this he arrived at interpretations such as would have done credit to Wieland Wagner. Here is an example of Felsenstein's depth psychology: why did Carmen reject Don José so abruptly in act 3? "She stands in desperation between her indissoluble ties to José and her disappointment—intensified to the point of hatred—that he does not measure up to the idol which emerged when she began to love him. Who is this idol?—Someone who doesn't exist." How about Escamillo? "No, he is not it. For there is only one. That, precisely is the tragedy or, if you prefer, the tragi-comedy. For her, José took the place—unconsciously of course—of the idolized Escamillo. This sounds absurd, but is the inevitable psychological fact without which the progress of the plot would be neither logical nor tragic."[7] What is a Carmen interpreter to do with such preposterous theories? How can something like that be acted out? Bizet certainly is no help. Alban Berg would have had to intervene here. Carmen—Lulu?

Felsenstein also spent some idle time finding out the financial conditions of bullfighters, arriving at the conclusion that these desperados earn millions and own villas and yachts. But again, what has that got to do with Bizet's Escamillo? Stanislavsky used to wrack his brains over such matters; for Shakespeare's *Othello* he researched the wealth of Roderigo's parents. Furthermore, with Felsenstein the smugglers' chief, Dancairo, became a key figure. He ruled his band with an iron fist, a sort of "Godfather." It seems that Bizet's score has unforeseen depths to which the directors refer again and again when dealing with a libretto not written by Mérimée.

In 1959 Wieland Wagner set his sights on this opera in Hamburg.[8] In Wieland's case one was never safe from surprises. Nor did he disappoint us this time. He put a *Carmen* on the stage that was aimed at making us radically forget all memories of the original work. Wieland had been in Spain, he had visited Seville, but he found the city was better suited for Rossini's barber shop than for *Carmen*. Therefore: no Spanish city life! All folklore was anathema. Wieland decided on an abstract no-man's-land with seats for the cigarette girls arranged in a semicircle, with a sentry box and a streetlight. A pale, grayish pink prevailed in the scene. Wieland found in poverty one of the dominant aspects of the work. Carmen was of "abject poverty"; the cigarette girls were "half-starved"; the urchins were half-naked. The chorus was drilled. Since they all sang the same melody in unison, they also moved in unison. There was no individuality. Seville was cleared of scenic clutter; this happened before to Nuremberg in Wieland's Bayreuth production. In the succeeding decors bloodred accents pointed toward the murderous finale. Wieland had found the key to the *Carmen* "mystery"; Eros Thanatos!

In the new production at the Vienna Staatsoper (1966) French was the language, and a return was made to Guiraud's recitatives. At times conservatism is also a virtue. Otto Schenk was the director; Günther Schneider-Siemssen created the decors. There was a happy reunion with Spain. A motley crew teemed on the Seville plaza. The same interest in details ruled in Vienna as in East Berlin. The children's parody of the changing of the guard was also Felsenstein's idea. The designer had moved the last act under the bleachers of the stadium, which favored Schenk's verism.

The very same year von Karajan presented his version of *Carmen* in the Grosse Festspielhaus in Salzburg. Again Guiraud triumphed. It was to be expected that a super-Seville would be exhibited on this enormous stage. There was so much to be seen that it was difficult to concentrate on the music. This was true especially since the maestro had decided to celebrate *Carmen* with the finesse of a chamber concert, which could hardly be brought into accord with the naturalistic bustle on the stage. A "soft" *Carmen* sounded from the orchestra pit, a dulcified score, and I am not sure that the composer would have objected. Teo Otto had moved the tavern of the second act to the seashore. It was an elegant smugglers' den, more like a bar of the Club Méditerranée, and Carmen appeared in suitably opulent attire. Of course, such an exclusive nightclub must have something to offer its clientele. This time our emcee decided on the assistance of the Mariemma Ballet de Espagna, for which he made dance music available from the fourth act (where it is definitely superfluous). The third act also played on the shore and, as far as the prevailing darkness allowed, we could make out a whole army of smugglers.

In 1967 Kurt Horres laid hands on Bizet in Wuppertal. He is an enthusiastic "alienator." It was to be anticipated that his *Carmen* would have nothing in common with the inherited image of that opera. No trace of the Spain where rich and not-so-rich Germans buy their condominiums. On stage, a confusion of stairs and grills. Little light, little love tragedy. Instead allusions to the Mafia (Dancairo), to fascism (the children's drill), and the Prussian goose step (soldiers). Felsenstein's new version with the dialogues formed the basic text. Again an attempt to "harden" *Carmen*. But was it still *Carmen*?

In 1972 the Metropolitan Opera (Lincoln Center, New York) presented a new *Carmen*, in French, with shortened dialogues, which caused one lady to remark to another: "The dialogue is coming across beautifully. I do wish I understood French." Goeran Gentele, who had been commissioned to attend to the mise-en-scène, was killed in an auto accident. Bodo Igesz, the stopgap, was not to be envied. Gentele had already made preparations for the production, had hired the stars, and decided on the stage designer Josef Svoboda, a fanatic of lighting and geometry. His image of Seville was typical: blocks of white walls in tropical sunshine, which, it was said, required 250,000 watts. In contrast was the monstrous mountain landscape of the third act, wrapped in nocturnal darkness. Svoboda took a dim view of the lighting installations at the Met: the apparatus available was not sufficient for the realization of his model plans. He also griped about the golden proscenium: it should have been painted black! Incidentally, Svoboda was not much in evidence during the rehearsals; he once had

103

to travel quickly to Prague, then he appeared again at the Met for a week, only to take off for Hamburg even before the premiere. Contractual obligations! They do not always agree with artistic work. At the end, Marilyn Horne's singing and Leonard Bernstein's conducting saved the evening.

Some of the *Carmen* first-nighters of 1972 still remembered the Jean-Louis Barrault Met production of 1967, with decors by Jacques Dupont. That scandal was said to have cost a quarter of a million dollars. The result was a danced *Carmen*. Everybody danced that evening: the factory girls, the street urchins, the soldiers, even the conductor. A universal fiesta mood prevailed. Hips were wriggled, sombreros were whirled into the azure sky, Florida oranges were hurled about. At the end of each production number a *tableau vivant charmant*! Applause, please! *Carmen* could not have been done "softer." It came close to emasculation. Barrault had simply seen too many musicals and believed that he had to cater to "the American taste." He underestimated the opera audience. He should have been hired for *Carmen Jones*.

The summer of 1977 saw a new *Carmen* at the Edinburgh Festival. Piero Faggioni produced the opera in the Oeser version on a stage of modest proportions, almost like a chamber play. The singers had read Mérimée and therefore could present characterizations rich in nuances. During long rehearsals everything was thought through and motivated to the last detail. Felsenstein would have applauded and made the discovery that even artists with voices such as Teresa Berganza's and Placido Domingo's can act convincingly.

The Tales of Hoffmann

Offenbach died before he could finish his opera; he was given enough time to complete the piano arrangement. He did not even begin the orchestration, and his friend Ernest Guiraud prepared the score. The premiere took place at the Opéra Comique in 1881, but without the Giulietta act. Jules Barbier's libretto, based on a "fantastic" play coauthored with Michel Carré, *Les Contes d'Hoffmann*, contained extensive prose dialogues which Guiraud condensed and changed, mostly to recitatives. The librettist had provided for the appearance of the poet's Muse in the framework story localized in Lutter's cellar tavern. She was Hoffmann's "true" love, the one who cured him in the end and liberated him from his obsessional love for the singer Stella. The character of this prima donna was not especially detailed, but Barbier may have thought that she combined traits of Olimpia, Giulietta, and Antonia. In the course of the years, the Muse disappeared from the opera, and Hoffmann ended up as an alcoholic. In the "Vienna version" for which Gustav Mahler was responsible, Stella was sacrificed, for Mahler showed no interest in the prologue and the epilogue. The Viennese version sanctioned the sequence Olimpia-Giulietta-Antonia. Nobody asked what Barbier and Offenbach had really intended.

This question was first posed by Hans Gregor who, in 1905, opened his newly founded Komische Oper in Berlin with *The Tales of Hoffmann*. With justified skepsis, Gregor and his director, Maximilian Moris, faced the score, disfigured as it was by deletions. Gregor wanted to track down the original version and decided to search in the Paris archives.

He did not find Offenbach's piano transcription there; it was probably destroyed during the fire at the Opéra Comique. But Gregor's Paris expedition was a success inasmuch as it brought to light two forgotten arias which were incorporated in the Berlin production: the spectacles aria of Coppelius and the diamond aria of Dapertutto. Gregor had no use for the Muse. Stella became Hoffmann's fourth worthless adventure in love, and there was nothing left for the hero but to drown his sorrow in drink. At the Komische Oper the Venetian act became the pièce de résistance. It determined the success of the opera, which lasted four hundred performances. The barcarole found its visual analogy in Karl Walser's decor, about which Fritz Jacobsohn raved as follows: "A deep blue, star-spangled, Italian night sky looked down on the love scene that was sweetened by the enchanting melody of the barcarole. Under a wide loggia, resplendent in soft, reddish light, the blissful couples swayed. From the canal that flowed under a high bridge cooing sounds beckoned from gondolas. . . . Venetian red, rich gold, greenish moonlight and in the background the silhouette of sleeping Venice."[1] The subscribers were convinced that what they saw and heard was Offenbach's legacy.

Arthur Maria Rabenalt, when he prepared his production in Darmstadt (1928), found in Stella the key to the action. In the evening Stella sang Mozart's Donna Anna while Hoffmann revealed his amorous experiences. She became the embodiment of the eternal feminine that continued to attract Hoffmann. The other incarnations were called Olimpia, Giulietta, and Antonia. Lutter's cellar was conceived of as a theater restaurant. Rabenalt chose to divide his stage in two stories: above, the foyer of the theater; below, the cellar restaurant. During the intermission, the foyer filled with operagoers, among them students who climbed down into the cellar for refreshment. Fascinated by the tales of Hoffmann, they did not return to *Don Giovanni*. At the end of the opera (Mozart's and Offenbach's) Stella appeared, first in the foyer, before she descended and sneered at the drunken Hoffmann. She left on Lindorf's arm. The divided stage was used throughout: above, Olimpia's room, and below, Spalanzani's ballroom; above, Giulietta's boudoir, and below, the Venetian portico; above, Antonia's private world, and below, Krespel's middle-class milieu.

In 1929 Ernst Legal thoroughly de-romanticized the opera (Krolloper, Berlin). It became fair game. L. Moholy-Nagy, a Bauhaus disciple and defender of the "total theater," designed the scenery. Lutter's cellar had steel furniture which added to the discomfort of the students in 1830. A spiral staircase led to Lindorf's elevated seat. Anyone who could not feel the *Biedermeier* atmosphere was dismissed by the Bauhaus adherents as a beer-swilling philistine. In any case, it was not the kind of atmosphere in which one would tell intimate love stories, and the martini cocktail had not yet been invented. Spalanzani's workshop came close to satisfying the fantastic element of the first episode. The spectator was transposed into a laboratory where the attempt was made to breathe life into mechanical dolls; it was a sterile test-tube world for which there was no equivalent in the music. Venice was also hygienic. Even sexual pleasure was sterilized. A few long-legged call girls swayed on swings. There was no gondola romance. Jacobsohn could not have warmed up to that ambiance. Finally, a studio apartment for Antonia, with movie effects. For spectators who did not find Offenbach's music sufficiently demonic, there were projections of Dr. Miracle's satanic eyes and clawed fingers. Thus the creeps were introduced.

The same audience that on 12 February 1929 was enchanted by the Bauhaus experiment cheered again on 28 November 1931, when Max Reinhardt produced the opera in the Grosse Schauspielhaus as supershow. The work appeared in new guise. Egon

Friedell and Hanns Sassmann had written a new text with thirteen scenes; Leo Blech had prepared the musical revision; Oskar Strnad was responsible for the decor. The wide-screen stage of the super-dimensional house troubled the artist. He was forced to look for frontal solutions instead of depth effects. The architect also changed the rigid aspect of the auditorium, so that the audience upon entrance found itself transposed into the *Biedermeier* of Old Berlin. The spectacle began on the square in front of the opera house with a comic coachman. It ended on the same opera square with a despairing Hoffmann, who had lost his Stella while the students honored her with a torch parade. In the penultimate scene Hoffmann had tried to abduct Stella, which led to a theater riot. For the Giulietta act, Reinhardt employed the revolving stage. The audience was invited to a gondola ride on the Canale Grande. At the sound of the barcarole Strnad's Venetian palaces, marked by decay, moved past. There was also a masquerade in the manner of Callot. The Muse was deleted. Four singers were used for Hoffmann's four loves. The Antonia of Jarmila Novotna is unforgettable. Never since has there been a more touching one. Reinhardt's spectacle had 174 performances. We had the chance to enjoy Reinhardt's Indian summer.

As was the case with *Carmen*, Walter Felsenstein had the ambition to restore the "Ur-version" of Offenbach. He wanted to cleanse the picture of the opera, free it from layers of varnish and touch-ups that were painted over it by alien hands. The restorer went about his work methodically. He sent a delegation to Paris, to uncover material that would bring him close to Offenbach. The yield was not inconsiderable. Felsenstein received the libretto of the premiere, the piano arrangement of the original performance, and the text of the *drame phantastique* by MM. Barbier and Carré (Odéon, 1851).

The director decided on a revision. The German standard text was jejune. Felsenstein replaced it with a new one, predominantly in iambics. The inspiration came from the Barbier-Carré *drame*. What the Komische Oper in East Berlin (1958) offered was a drama with musical interludes. Offenbach had found a new Barbier. After eliminating Guiraud's recitatives, much prose was spoken in Felsenstein's version. Occasionally, there was melodramatic background music. This brings us to the crux of the arrangement. Felsenstein showed little respect for Offenbach's music. He mistrusted Offenbach's musical as well as dramatic instincts, and did not hesitate to dismember both trios in the Antonia act to make the music comply with the new text, according to the principle *primo le parole, dopo la musica.* Without reluctance he transposed the largo part of the second duet of Giulietta and Hoffmann to the end of the opera where he needed apotheosis music for the Muse. Offenbach characterized his dramatis personae through the music he wrote for them. For Hoffmann's love for Antonia he created one special musical world, unmistakable and not interchangeable; for the relationship between Hoffmann and Giulietta another, again a unique one. Felsenstein had no ear for that. He made high-handed exchanges and used the allegretto part of the Hoffmann-Antonia duet as love duet for Hoffmann and—Giulietta.

Felsenstein investigated Hoffman's "initial situation:" why, he asked, would the poet tell those three awful stories to the students at Lutter's tavern? His answer: he wanted to forget Stella, who at that moment was singing Donna Anna at the Berlin Opera. His stories, according to Felsenstein, were "born in pain, revengefulness, and desire." The Hoffmann of this revision did not end up in an alcoholic daze, cursing love. The Muse of poetry prevented such an inglorious ending. She became Felsenstein's key figure. As in the Barbier-Carré version, she first appeared in the prologue and there, in full view of everybody, turned into the tutelary spirit Niklaus. In the end the Muse intervened once more and reminded Hoffmann of his true mission as poet. I found this solution rather "bourgeois." If one has had bad luck as a lover, it does not follow that one has to write poetry right away. Only dilettantes would do that. E. T. A. Hoffmann would have had objections to such an untragic solution. He hated the philistines and respected the intrusion of the demonic into the real world. The conventional end of Offenbach's Hoffmann in the throes of delirium tremens is, in any case, more Hoffmannesque than the solution offered by Barbier-Carré-Felsenstein. Incidentally, the traditional ending had a stunning effect in the Krolloper. Lindorf pointed to the drunken Hoffmann, whereupon Stella reacted with a "Fie!" and took Lindorf's arm. Hoffmann's last outcry was for Stella as she, too, slipped away from him. Those condemned to a tragic existence cannot be soothed by the balm of a muse. Felsenstein completely distorted the character of Antonia. She became a hysteric seeking death, although the music does not sustain such a caricature. Giulietta died in her boudoir, poisoned by Dapertutto. Critics had made fun of the gondola trip in the "Circus Reinhardt." But let us not overlook that Rudolf Heinrich had to design in East Berlin for the Giulietta act no fewer than four scenes, which put a heavy load on the fragile barcarole. First there was a palace façade with gondoliers; then the ballroom; next the private salon of the courtesan; and finally the court of the palace. A supershow which Felsenstein placed after the Antonia act because, as he once said, the Giulietta experience was the most devastating one for Hoffmann.

It is worth mentioning that Felsenstein's restoration benefited from the previous work done in the fifties by Otto Maag and Hans Haug. These two pioneers had already elevated the Muse to be Hoffmann's guiding star, and had predestined her as early as the prologue to become the *dea ex machina*.

The Stuttgart staging of 1965 may be descibed as conservative, but by no means in a negative sense. The traditional sequence was observed: Olimpia, Giulietta, Antonia. The Muse not only appeared as consoler at the end, but in the beginning, where, as in the original play, she climbed out of a wine barrel, a sort of tutelary spirit. Lindorf had the chance to introduce himself as rival with his often-deleted aria. Dapertutto's song was addressed to a diamond and no longer to a reflecting mirror. The Venetian sextet was rescued, and the four female roles were entrusted to one superb singer (Anja Silja). The poor German of the translation was retained. Otto Schenk's directing was again excellent workmanship. Günther Schneider-Siemssen's scenery exuded Romanticism. Everything was tasteful, far removed from experimentation. The objection can be made that in the end Hoffmann, quill in hand,

The Tales of Hoffmann

began to write poetry, which hardly differed from Felsenstein's kiss of the Muse.

The production at the Munich Theater am Gärtnerplatz (1966) more or less relied on the Maag-Haug version: Hoffmann renounced Stella and from then on devoted himself to his poetic mission. Because a final aria was needed for Hoffmann's new aspirations, the problem was solved by borrowing his B-major largo from the Giulietta act. The Venice act, placed at the end of the scurrilous trilogy, was also diminished musically by the deletion of the sextet. This time Giulietta died by Schlemihl's hand: he stabbed her. The Antonia concept was again in contrast to the music: the director, Kurt Pscherer, saw her as an egotist incapable of love, while Offenbach never poured forth sweeter melodies than here. To be sure, if these enchanting airs are dismissed as mere tearjerkers, then such blunders occur.

In Wiesbaden, the very same year, they tried to do better. Václas Kašlik was engaged as director and Josef Svoboda as designer. The Czech duo worked almost exclusively with projections and mirror effects, such as were tried out first in Prague with the Laterna Magica. Then and now technical tricks diverted from the emotional power of the opera. This might still have been acceptable in the Olimpia act, which hardly has a realistic basis. But Lutter's cellar and the Antonia episode are firmly rooted in reality, and a production that is surreal from the start weakens the intrusion of the irrational when it finally occurs. The Antonia act must start as a middle-class idyll. It says so in the score. The demons are only released by Dr. Miracle. That, too, is in the score.

Of all distortions to which the opera was exposed on the stage, the Paris version was the worst (Palais Garnier, 1974). Patrice Chéreau and his stage designer, Richard Peduzzi, were responsible for this corruption. Lutter's cellar was demolished, perhaps bombed out, and in its place there was a whores' hangout where Hoffmann delved into his memories before he ended in a drunken stupor. Chéreau had changed the sequence of the acts without valid reason. He began with Giulietta, put Olimpia in the middle, and ended with Antonia—whose mother, by the way, was a prostitute whom we had met before, in Venice, in Giulietta's company. There were other strange alienations. The Antonia act began with a funeral. Olimpia did not sing her aria: her (?) voice came over a loudspeaker. The mechanical doll actually did disintegrate. A strange gentleman in black, who had made a timid debut in Reinhardt's production, now spooked through the Paris opera, once on horseback, then in a coach, obviously Death personified. Even snobbish habitués could not overlook that. All this was presented in a permanent setting, somewhere at the periphery of a surrealist port or industrial city of hostile chill. Good old Offenbach, who moved among the plutocrats, could not have helped shivering at this transformation of his musical visions.

The Viennese were used to enjoying "their" *Hoffmann* in the following form: a prelude with a chorus of drunken students who asked Hoffmann to sing them a song and tell them stories from his macabre love life. The Olimpia episode made the beginning. Then followed the Giulietta act, and Antonia concluded the series. The students were still drinking during the epilogue. Hoffmann already lay under the table when Stella appeared with Lindorf, and expressed her scorn for the alcoholic.

Vienna became acquainted with a new version in 1976. Dr. Fritz Oeser, who had earned success when reestablishing the "original" *Carmen*, now had the ambition to give Offenbach's posthumous opera the form which might have been in the mind of the moribund composer. Dr. Oeser spent weeks in Paris archives and discovered new sketches in Offenbach's hand. He found new material for the role of the Muse and additional music for the Giulietta act. Dr. Oeser did not hesitate to appropriate melodies from Offenbach's *Die Rheinnixen*. After all, the composer himself had taken the barcarole from his unsuccessful opera, where it had served as "elf song."

Oeser's revised version was the basis for the production in the Vienna Volksoper. Johannes Schaaf was the director. He and his designer, Ernst Fuchs, had the unfortunate idea to retain throughout the evening Lutter's cellar as a framework. This led to the permanent presence of Hoffmann's drinking companions—a gimmick bound to disturb illusion. However, Oeser's revision deserves another chance: it belongs in the hands of a director who loves the romantic.

The Festspiele in Salzburg opened their 1980 season with a production of *The Tales of Hoffmann*, a centenary tribute to the composer who died in 1880. Conductor James Levine and director/designer Jean-Pierre Ponnelle gave birth to a new version, which is indebted to both the traditional French Choudens edition and Oeser's recent restorative labors. Offenbach's *Tales* is a rather intimate opera which could only lose on Salzburg's enormous stage as it had suffered in Reinhardt's Berlin circus in 1931. To overcome the spatial exigencies in Salzburg, Ponnelle worked with a tripartite stage which allowed for scenic hocus-pocus left and right of the central action. After checking with his wife, the tired businessman seemed to enjoy the spectacle in which, by the way, the Giulietta episode was given the third slot. Hoffmann's beloveds were portrayed by one singer, Edda Moser. *"Trois femmes dans la même femme,"* as the libretto has it. Placido Domingo, vocally very comfortable, looked the part of a tormented romantic poet. In the epilogue, the Muse, usually spurned in older productions, was in full command of the situation and ready to comfort Hoffmann.

Der Rosenkavalier

This "comedy for music" has its roots in the soil of Vienna, the 1910 art-nouveau Vienna of Hofmannsthal as well as the Vienna of Maria Theresa. The first night took place in Dresden (1911), the site of the *Salome* and *Electra* premieres. The participation of two Austrians guaranteed the success of the opera in the Saxon capital. Alfred Roller created the scenery and costumes. Max Reinhardt was called in because the director-in-residence, Georg Toller, was at a loss when he found himself confronted with this new form of musical theater. Unfortunately, Reinhardt's directing can no longer be recaptured in detail. Strauss tells us in his reminiscences that the singers came as "accomplished actors to the rehearsal" after Reinhardt had coached them, and Strauss continues: "The result was a new style of opera and a perfect performance."[1] After the composer had left Dresden, conductor Ernst von Schuch began to delete parts of the score (he was a passionate deleter), and Strauss could do nothing but protest.

Three months after the Dresden premiere, *Der Rosenkavalier* appeared in the Vienna Hofoper. Roller repeated his Dresden mise-en-scène. With a watchful eye Hofmannsthal followed the rehearsals, which were conducted by Wilhelm von Wymetal. The evening of 8 April 1911 turned out to be a triumph for Strauss and the Vienna Opera, where *Der Rosenkavalier* has lost none of its luster since. To be sure, there were the compulsive carpers. Julius Korngold, then critic of the *Neue Freie Presse*, was among them, and he was the densest. Narrow-mindedly, he tore the score and libretto to pieces.[2] He could not possibly have known at the time that his son Erich would learn a great deal from Strauss, and that Erich would not have much luck with his librettists.

The early stage career of the opera need not concern us here. However, two episodes deserve to be mentioned. In Berlin, Strauss had bad experiences with the general manager, Georg von Hülsen, who had the nerve to "purge" the opera of sexual allusions to make it presentable at court. If Strauss had not threatened to withdraw his work, von Hülsen would have sacrificed the Baron's sexual exploits to please the chaste ears of the empress.

The stormy evening in the Milan Scala is also part of this opera's early history. The Italians could enjoy a Viennese waltz only on ballet evenings; in an opera they resented the three-quarter time that dominates the end of the second act and the first half of the third. It seemed for a while as though the booing would kill the opera. Then came the trio, which assured the success of the opera. Strauss and his wife in their box could smile again.

Now on to the actual production problems: the publisher, A. Fürstner, at first forced the theaters to acquire Roller's decors and costumes together with the score; *Der Rosenkavalier* was a package deal. This meant that for years the opera was protected against directorial experimentation. For the audiences between the two world wars the Roller settings remained sacrosanct, especially so since it seemed that the artist had found a definitive visual form that was in absolute agreement with Hofmannsthal's stage directions—a perfect mixture of rococo and *Jugendstil*. Roller saw the Princess's bedroom with Hofmannsthal's eyes: To the left, in the alcove, the great, tentlike canopy bed. Next to it, a Chinese screen. Further, a sofa and a few chairs. The dominant color was golden yellow; the furniture was upholstered in pink. The reception room at von Faninal's, elegant but not ostentatious. A refined splendor. That nouveau riche had taste. The walls were cream-colored, the wainscoting red as were the fireplaces and door frames. Finally, the private room in the inn. A table set for two. In the background left, an alcove with a bed. A comfortable place. The Baron did not have to be apologetic: he had used the room frequently, although on previous occasions it had no trapdoors, no treacherous sliding walls.

The harmony Roller had achieved between scenery, action, and music was questioned by succeeding directors and their stage designers. *Der Rosenkavalier* also fell victim to experimentation. A. M. Rabenalt (Würzburg, 1927) proposed a "uniform scenic architecture." It was supposed to be assembled from "variable compositional modules" which would present a new configuration in each act. The modules consisted of "hollow, rotating cylinders whose circular cross sections simulated a baroque character." The director insisted that, within this abstract form, he could accentuate a "subtle chamber-play realism."[3]

Hofmannsthal once pointed out that the Nuremberg of 1500 as an urban unit carries the action of *Die Meistersinger*, while the 1740 Vienna of Maria Theresa sustains the action of *Der Rosenkavalier*. Hofmannsthal created, as he himself expressed it, "a real and therefore credible total urban world with hundreds of living interrelations." A mechanical standardized stage, such as was in Rabenalt's mind, is simply not up to such a task.

In 1960, the Grosse Festspielhaus in Salzburg opened with *Der Rosenkavalier*. Rudolf Hartmann as director and Teo Otto as designer had the thankless job of producing on Holzmeister's superstage what is basically an intimate "comedy for music." Otto decided to make the wide stage for the second and third acts manageable by adding side balconies. A black cyclorama closed off the upstage in both instances. In the second act the duenna did not take her place at the customary window but on a balcony, from where she described Rofrano's arrival. In the last act the Princess retired to the balcony and stared into the darkness while the Baron made his unceremonious exit. Since the performance was blessed with an excellent ensemble of singers, and von Karajan, with the Vienna Philharmonic Orchestra, knew how to translate into sound the most subtle stirrings of the soul, the evening turned into a festival after all. The composer had benefited greatly from a libretto that created "space for music," for what separated the characters and what united them. It is up to the director to realize this "musical space," an assignment which, in Salzburg, could not be carried out for reasons of—space. Thus our thoughts went back to Roller's intimacy where there was no room for megalomania.

The Covent Garden *Rosenkavalier* (1966) left us with mixed feelings. There the movie director, Luchino Visconti, had one of his gimmicky evenings. Hofmannsthal-Strauss ended the first act with a Princess steeped in melancholy meditation, "supporting her head with her hand," as demanded by both stage directions and the music. Not so Visconti, who had his Princess pace up and down restlessly until, on arriving at the apron, she heaved a big sigh. The conclusion of the second act brought another directorial innovation: the Baron hurled his wineglass to the floor. At the end of the opera the little blackamoor expressed his pleasure over the found handkerchief with a whoop. These were the enhanced endings. Other peculiarities cropped up. Although in the beginning there was a bed on stage, the amorous couple evidently had preferred to make love on pillows in front of an open fire. Before the Baron entered, the pointless bed disappeared. In the levee and pub scenes Visconti repeated the whole roster of *lazzi* so dear to his forebears. Ferdinando Scarfiotti's scenery was a styleless medley of Roman baroque, art nouveau, and *Biedermeier*.

In Wiesbaden (1967) *Der Rosenkavalier* was identified as a "dream play." The stage was kept dark. Only strange reflexes flickered. The rococo had disappeared; fin de siècle ruled. Evidently we were dealing with a rather decadent society. Director C. H. Drese attacked the comedy as if he were still mesmerized by *Electra*. What was not supposed to happen to the Baron until the third act—namely, his loss of self-assurance—happened at the end of the second act. Only a very confused director could hit on the idea of dividing the third act into different scenes. The trio and duet were transposed into a bucolic landscape; the private dining room was dissolved, and we were in a kind of baroque pleasure garden that the designer, Frank Schulte, had envisioned. We shall shortly encounter another "dream-play" attempt.

In the meantime we can recuperate in Vienna and New York. In 1968 the Vienna Staatsoper acquired a new *Rosenkavalier*. Otto Schenk, the stage director, was essentially faithful to the tradition and invented new gags only for the burlesque scenes. Rudolf Heinrich had moved the canopy bed to the foreground, thereby reducing the space for the levee. Bernstein conducted, paid little attention to the text, and was entranced by the sound of the orchestra. It is regrettable that the record industry failed to give permanency to this ravishing interpretation.

In 1969, the Metropolitan Opera revived *Der Rosenkavalier*. It was in the best tradition, worth seeing and hearing. Böhm conducted, Nathaniel Merrill directed. No gags, no gimmicks. One could sigh with relief. It seemed as though time stood still. Robert O'Hearn had supplied the milieu. The large room in the second act was too ostentatious, though optically a pièce de résistance and duly applauded by the audience. It was a scenic wonderwork, complete with ceiling frescos, as if an Elector lived here and not Herr von Faninal who, though nouveau riche, did not have unlimited financial resources at his disposal. Designer O'Hearn had taken his inspiration from the marble hall and huge staircase of Weissenstein castle. After all, that was Austrian baroque with which J. L. von Hildebrand had made a prince happy. The ground plan of the *chambre séparée* was so complicated that the singers had difficulties finding their way around.

In 1972 Otto Schenk was invited to repeat his Vienna success in the Nationaltheater, Munich. The production was the event of the year, especially since Carlos Kleiber (like his father before him) elicited from the orchestra the very last drop of tonal finesse. Jürgen Rose created the decor, enchanting rococo pleasure rooms, inspired this time by Nymphenburg castle. He blundered in the third act, however, when he moved the *chambre séparée* into an attic. A seedier background for the Baron's most recent adventure could not be invented. To be sure, the man was not choosy. But the Princess could not be expected to climb the stairs to an attic. A loft for the ecstasy of the trio and the intimacy of the duet! The ladies had a hard time singing of love and renunciation against such a background.

In one of her depressed hours Hofmannsthal's Princess feels "the frailty of all that is temporal; how everything runs through one's fingers, everything dissolves that we try to grasp, everything melts into thin air like a mist and a dream." Her words could be used as a motto for the *Rosenkavalier* production that Joachim Herz and Rudolf Heinrich had planned for the Paris Opéra in 1970. It was never staged because of those notorious organizational difficulties, though since the director had published his concept, we may discuss it. Again we land in a sort of "dream play."[4] Herz and Heinrich had proposed to do away with plastic architecture, using screens instead. These screens, moved by visible lackeys or invisible stagehands, were supposed to determine the floor plan and the ambiance of every act. Pale green and gold was the color scheme for the first act; white and silver for the second; the inn was assigned a brown. These screens were supposed to appear within each act in various configurations. In the second act, for instance, they first narrowed the space and thus formed a sort of dressing room for Sophie, where the lady's maids were still busy with last-minute adjustments of her dress, while the duenna stood on a laundry basket and, looking through an opening of her screen into the auditorium, described the arrival of Rofrano. Later on, these screens separated and opened the view upstage for the arrival of the Rosenkavalier.

Valzacchi and his helpers were supposed to assemble the decor while the third act had already started: the walls were just being erected, a ceiling was suspended, the bed was prepared. In the course of the evening the Baron would have been exposed to sheer bedlam. Here are a few ideas from Herz's scenario: there was a washing facility complete with bidet; a supernumerary came out of the lavatory, barefoot and in his shirt, but with his hat on. He carried his pants in his hands. From two holes in the wall "two rickety female arms" appeared and grabbed the Baron. One extra had an epileptic fit. Another had crawled under the sofa which later began to move. The dining table moved likewise. When the Baron opened the bed curtain, he found a hanged man dangling above the bed. Skulls and other accessories for a "Horror House" were also supplied. When Hofmannsthal wrote his "Viennese masquerade" he certainly was not thinking of the Prater.

During the Baron's departure the screens were supposed to move in three-quarter time before they finally disappeared. This created a "free space in the moonlight." From here the Princess would have left in a coach with Herr von Faninal. Then the blackamoor would come to be hoisted on a rope to take his place in a "comedians' box." We have not yet mentioned these comedians, though they were an essential part of the director's concept. Heinrich worried about the ceiling of his screen stage. Total emptiness was out of the question. How about allusions to the baroque and the Italian commedia dell'arte? Splendid, thought Heinrich, and created a lateral connection between the side parts of the proscenium: three balconies, of which the middle one projected into the auditorium. Up here on Olympus lived the forebears of the "Vienna masquerade" that was being acted out on the stage below, an assortment of commedia figures, stuffed dolls representing Harlequin, Columbina, Pantalone. There was also a little blackamoor whom the one on the stage joined when he was pulled up at the end of the opera. Behind these waxworks were frescos à la Maulpertsch. Up here the blessed spirits of the eighteenth century foregathered and looked down, without envy, on the cerebral games of the sick twentieth.

The Parisians did not get to see the Herz-Heinrich version of this opera. They were "recompensed" when director Rudolf Steinböck and designer Ezio Frigerio gave the opera a face-lifting in 1976. This, too, showed no trace of what Hofmannsthal had envisaged. It began with a monstrous bed, centrally located, although its function was exhausted after the brief orchestra prelude. For the levee a curtain was drawn, opening up the view on the façade of a palace, an irrational background for the accomplishments (or blunders) of a hairdresser. For the second act a palace for Faninal was erected which not even Prince Eugene could have afforded. In Paris they did not know what to do with the tavern. The name of Watteau was far more inspiring, and so the final scene was transposed into a Watteau landscape. The Baron evidently remembered his "Bohemian Nights" and had a yen for a fête champêtre. "Just be sure there's some hay nearby."

Thus *Der Rosenkavalier* also became a victim of directorial arrogance. We were just foolish enough to consider this opera invulnerable.

Coda

Musiktheater—when Lotte Lehmann's Marschallin bewailed the process of aging in front of the mirror; when Hans Hotter's Wotan confided his innermost feelings to his daughter; when Richard Mayr's King Marke lamented Tristan's betrayal: we were in the presence of *Musiktheater*, created only by voices guided by artistic intelligence, and no director could claim credit.

Notes

Cadenza

1. Oskar Bie, *Die Oper* (Berlin, 1920), p. 9.

Don Giovanni

1. Quoted by Alfred Roller in his article "Mahler und die Inszenierung," *Musikblätter des Anbruch* 2 (April 1920): 365.
2. Richard Specht, *Gustav Mahler* (Berlin, 1913), p. 139.
3. Bruno Walter, *Thema und Variationen* (Stockholm, 1947), p. 253.
4. Ernst Lert, *Mozart auf dem Theater* (Berlin, 1918), p. 385.
5. Max Slevogt, "Meine Inszenierung des Don Giovanni," *Melos* 4, no. 3 (1 October 1924): 174.
6. Oscar Fritz Schuh, *Salzburger Dramaturgie* (Vienna, 1951), p. 44.
7. Alfred Einstein, *Mozart* (Stockholm, 1947), p. 573.
8. Franz Willnauer and Oscar Fritz Schuh, *Bühne als geistiger Raum* (Bremen, 1963), p. 80.
9. E. T. A. Hoffmann, "Don Juan," no. 4 of *Phantasiestücke in Callot's Manier*, reprinted in his *Sämtliche poetische Werke* (Berlin, 1963), 1:78–79.
10. Einstein, *Mozart*, p. 573.
11. Walter Felsenstein, "Donna Anna und Don Giovanni," in his *Schriften zum Musiktheater* (Berlin, 1976), p. 381.
12. For the following, see ibid., pp. 379–83.

13. Siegfried Melchinger, "Die Bühne des 'Don Giovanni,' " *Jahrbuch der Komischen Oper* 7 (1966–67): 142.

14. K. H. Ruppel, *Grosse Stunden der Musik* (Munich, 1975), pp. 40–41.

15. See Rudolf Noelte, "Eine Nacht im Leben und Sterben des Don Giovanni," in *Oper 1974*, ed. Imre Fabian (Velber, 1974), pp. 6–11.

16. Götz Friedrich in an interview with Heinz Ludwig, *Oper 1974*, ed. Imre Fabian (Velber, 1974), p. 16.

17. Corsaro disclosed some of his directing principles in his article "A Small Matter of Survival," *New York Times*, 16 March 1969, p. D 19.

Così fan tutte

1. E. T. A. Hoffmann, "Die Serapions Brüder," in his *Sämtliche poetische Werke* (Berlin, 1963), 2: 90.

2. For the public reception of *Così*, see Hermann Abert, *W.A. Mozart* (Leipzig, 1921), 2: 643.

3. Götz Friedrich, "Zur Inszenierungskonzeption 'Così fan tutte,' " *Jahrbuch der Komischen Oper* 3 (1962–63): 34–56.

4. Richard Strauss *Betrachtungen und Erinnerungen* (Zürich, 1949), p. 103.

The Magic Flute

1. Mozart to his father, 13 October 1781, in *Gesamtausgabe der Briefe und Aufzeichnungen der Familie Mozart*, ed. Erich H. Müller von Asow (Berlin, 1942), 3:134.

2. Wolfgang Hildesheimer voices his low opinion of Schikaneder's libretto on pp. 326–30 of his biography *Mozart* (Frankfurt, 1980).

3. Götz Friedrich, *Die Zauberflöte in der Inszenierung Walter Felsensteins* (Berlin, 1958).

4. Ernst Bloch, "Die Zauberflöte und Symbole von heute," in his *Verfremdungen I* (Frankfurt, 1962), p. 100.

5. Arnold Zweig's article "Die reingestimmte Zauberflöte" was originally published in the East Berlin daily *Tägliche Rundschau* (23 March 1954). It is now easily accessible in Friedrich, *Zauberflöte*, pp. 201–2.

6. Johann Jakob Engel, the manager of the Berlin Nationaltheater, to King Friedrich Wilhem II of Prussia, quoted in Julius Kapp, *Geschichte der Staatsoper Berlin* (Berlin, n.d.), p. 23.

7. The painter's color schemes are recorded in F. Welz, ed., *Oscar Kokoschka, Designs of the Stage Settings for W.A. Mozart's Magic Flute* (Salzburg, 1955), pp. 57–64.

8. Richard Wagner, "Das Publikum in Zeit und Raum," in his *Sämtliche Schriften und Dichtungen* (Leipzig, n.d.), 10: 96.

Fidelio

1. Lotte Lehmann, *My Many Lives* (New York, 1948), p. 122.

2. Ibid., p. 123.

3. See Max Mell, *Alfred Roller* (Vienna, 1922), p. 27.

4. Adolf Weissmann in his *Fidelio* review in *B.Z. am Mittag*, 21 November 1927.

5. For the principles which guided Rabenalt in his Fidelio mise-en-scène, see Arthur Maria Rabenalt, *Oper in der Zeit* (Berlin, n.d.), pp. 280–85.

6. Friedrich Dieckmann, "Zu einem *Fidelio* 1970," *Theater der Zeit*, January 1970, pp. 6–11.

7. Günther Rennert, *Opernarbeit, Inszenierungen 1963–1973* (Munich, 1974), p. 91.

Der Freischütz

1. Quoted in Hans Schnoor, *Weber auf dem Welttheater* (Dresden, 1943), p. 114.

2. Arthur Maria Rabenalt, *Oper in der Zeit* (Berlin, n.d.), p. 275.

3. Adorno's ruminations were made available to the Frankfurt audiences in the program under the title "Bilderwelt des *Freischütz.*"

4. Weber's conversation with J. C. Lobe is quoted in part in the official Frankfurt program.

5. Karl Schönewolf, introduction to the Reclam edition of the libretto of *Der Freischütz* (Leipzig, 1951), p. 36.

6. See Felsenstein's conversation with Siegfried Melchinger in Walter Felsenstein, *Schriften zum Musiktheater* (Berlin, 1976), pp. 265–72.

7. Wolfgang Lange, "Montierte Collagen," *Theater der Zeit* 10 (October 1970): 22–25.

8. Quoted in Schönewolf, introduction, p. 36.

The Flying Dutchman

1. Richard Wagner, "Bemerkungen zur Aufführung der Oper 'Der fliegende Holländer,' " in his *Sämtliche Schriften und Dichtungen* (Leipzig, n.d.), 5: 160–63.

2. Arthur Maria Rabenalt, *Oper in der Zeit* (Berlin, n.d.), p. 296.

3. Antoine Goléa, *Gespräche mit Wieland Wagner* (Salzburg, 1968), p. 133.

4. The date of Wagner's letter is uncertain. For the German wording see Richard Wagner, *Sämtliche Briefe* (Leipzig, 1970), 1: 314.

Aida

1. Review by Richard Aldrich in *New York Times*, 17 November 1908, p. 16.

2. For Wieland Wagner's interpretation of *Aida* see Antoine Goléa, *Gespräche mit Wieland Wagner* (Salzburg, 1968), pp. 58–61.

3. Bohumil Herlischka, "Anmerkungen zur Inszenierung," in the program of the Frankfurt Opera.

4. Zimmermann's "metallic" stage is analyzed by Hans-Gerald Otto in *Jahrbuch der Komischen Oper* 9 (1968–69): 130–32.

Carmen

1. See Carl Hagemann, *Oper und Szene* (Berlin, 1905), pp. 278–91.
2. Fritz Jacobsohn, *Hans Gregor's Komische Oper 1905–1911* (Berlin, n.d.), p. 42.
3. Friedrich Nietzsche, "Aus dem Nachlass 1883/88: der Fall Wagner," in his *Werke* (Leipzig, 1923), 11: 183–84.
4. For Stanislavsky's work on *Carmen*, see G. Kristi, *Stanislavskis Weg zur Oper* (Berlin, 1954), pp. 170–86.
5. Tyrone Guthrie, *A Life in the Theatre* (London, 1959), p. 224.
6. Walter Felsenstein, "Die Tragödie der Carmen," in his *Schriften zum Musiktheater* (Berllin, 1976), pp. 238–43.
7. Ibid.
8. Wieland discusses his *Carmen* concept with Antoine Goléa, *Gespräche mit Wieland Wagner* (Salzburg, 1968), pp. 48–55.

The Tales of Hoffmann

1. Fritz Jacobsohn, *Hans Gregor's Komische Oper 1905–1911* (Berlin, n.d.), p. 26.

Der Rosenkavalier

1. Richard Strauss, *Betrachtungen und Erinnerungen* (Zürich, 1949), p. 234.
2. Julius Korngold, *Deutsches Opernschaffen der Gegenwart* (Leipzig, 1921), pp. 155–67.
3. Arthur Maria Rabenalt *Oper in der Zeit* (Berlin, n.d.), p. 326.
4. Joachim Herz and Rudolf Heinrich, "Entwurf einer 'Rosenkavalier'-Inszenierung," *Musikbühne 74* (Berlin, 1974), pp. 107–17.

Index of Names

129

Index of Names

Index of Names

Index of Names